# Lost London

# Lost London

## HERMIONE HOBHOUSE

Houghton Mifflin Company  Boston
1972

*For Harriet and Francis*

# Contents

## Acknowledgements

I have received a great deal of advice and help from many organisations and individuals, together with many suggestions for buildings to be included in this book. It would have been impossible to include all the interesting buildings lost in the last hundred years, but I have tried to compile a representative selection without any major omissions. Inevitably, readers who know their London well may regret the absence of some of their personal favourites.

Theatres and other centres of entertainment are so well covered elsewhere that I have ignored them deliberately, but I have tried to include all other categories of London buildings. I have also avoided commenting on the Whitehall and Covent Garden schemes, under discussion when this book went to press.

Lord Sandford, Parliamentary Under-Secretary of State at the Department of the Environment, was kind enough to see me, and to explain the problems involved in the preservation of historic buildings, as was Lord Kennet, his predecessor at the Ministry of Housing from 1966 to 1970.

I am most grateful to Lady Dartmouth, Chairman of the Greater London Council's Historic Buildings Board, who has done so much to preserve London's shrinking stock of historic buildings, both for her own help and that of her department, particularly that of Mr Ashley Barker, Surveyor of Historic Buildings. I have also drawn on the G.L.C.'s records and photographic collection, and I am most indebted to the generous help of Miss Mercer, Archivist to the Council, and her staff, particularly Miss Watson, the Photographic Librarian.

Much of the photographic material has come from the files of the National Monuments Record, and I must thank Mr Cecil Farthing and his staff, particularly Mr Nicholas Cooper, for a great deal of help, both in my research, and in providing superb illustrations, often from old and indifferent originals.

Mr Howgego of the Guildhall Library has given me much invaluable assistance, and a large number of illustrations are drawn from the City of London's collection. I have also received help from the Local History Collections of the City of Westminster, the Royal Borough of Kensington and Chelsea, and the Boroughs of Camden and Islington.

I am indebted to the Duke of Westminster for permission to use photographs from the Grosvenor Estate Office, and to the Duke of Bedford and the Trustees of the Bedford Estate for similar material. It would not have been possible to compile this book without access to the R.I.B.A. Drawings Collection and its Library, and I should like to thank Mr John Harris and his staff for their help.

I am indebted in many ways to the national preservation societies – the Society for the Protection of Ancient Buildings, the Georgian Group and the Victorian Society and their secretaries – for assistance and advice at all stages of this book, for access to their reports and records, and for many valuable suggestions. Finally, I must thank Julia Eccleshare and James de la Mare for help with picture research, and Caroline Hobhouse, Richard Hayes and Helen Whitten of Macmillan's for their help and encouragement.

H. H.

# INTRODUCTION

. . . the object of the work we have before us, is to make nobler and more humanly enjoyable the life of the great City whose existing record we seek to mark down; to preserve of it for her children and those yet to come whatever is best in her best or fairest in her present; to induce her municipalities to take the lead and stimulate among her citizens that historic and social conscience which to all great communities is their most sacred possession . . .

In these rolling periods C. R. Ashbee put forward, in 1901, the real arguments for the preservation of historic buildings and ancient streets, and despite their unfashionable Edwardian dress they are still valid today. The most important reason for retaining older buildings is not the antiquarian one but the improvement of the lives of present and future citizens.

The buildings lost in London over the last hundred years are a loss to us all, and a very great loss it has been. In 1928, Osbert Sitwell could write of 'a devastation of London more serious and widespread than the havoc caused by the Great Fire'; if to this we add the damage caused by the Blitz and the post-war reconstruction, then it is clear that the face of London has been more altered than that of any other comparable Western European capital in the same period.

This book, then, is primarily a catalogue of destruction, a list of buildings which were obsolescent or uneconomic, or stood in the way of progress in the form of a new road or a new bridge, or of an institution like a hospital or a university. Throughout the hundred years it covers there were voices raised against the destruction, merely deprecatory at first, but leading to the formation of pressure groups who gradually achieved legislative protection for historic buildings in London.

To prevent it becoming, in Gibbon's words, 'little more than the register of the crimes, follies and misfortunes' of the people of London in dealing with their environment, I have set out to do two other things. Firstly, I have gathered a pictorial record of some of the departed splendours – I hope a representative and catholic selection, though it must be a personal one.

The book could of course have been far longer, because of the tragically large selection of material available. I have deliberately excluded all but extremely significant buildings outside Central London, and I have included only one place of entertainment – the Crystal Palace. There are a number of fascinating vanished theatres and cinemas, but these are well covered in specialist volumes.

Secondly, though I have deliberately not commented on most of the new buildings I have tried to analyse the reasons behind the destruction, in the hope that this may avert further losses, and save something more for Macaulay's New Zealander than office blocks and mammoth hotels.

This is not to declare war on all redevelopment. This could only be done by someone ignorant of the history of London, which has included wave after wave of necessary and interesting rebuilding. It must be acknowledged that there are many good and sufficient social and economic reasons for the demolition of old buildings, and the retention of an outdated town plan or of too many obsolescent buildings cannot be allowed to make a strait jacket for the future which will stifle economic growth or inhibit the improvement of living conditions.

In many instances, indeed, the way in which a series of fine buildings has occupied the same site almost gives the lie to the preservationist case. On the other hand, how much richer would London be today, if some control had been exercised over demolition in the past hundred years.

## The Arguments for Preservation

'Sewers are in,' wrote the Editor of *The Builder* in 1849, 'and it is quite time they were.' Today we may say the same of conservation in its very widest sense, and for the same grim reasons that the Victorians concerned themselves with sewers and drains – that the environment is gradually becoming intolerable. The preservation of some historic areas of our cities and some of our more important buildings is only one aspect of this fight, which must involve every aspect of national planning, from controlling the population to allocating resources among motorways and national parks, urban renewal and new towns.

Preservation in this context is probably best defined as the retention of a building or an area with as many of its historic features, and as nearly in its original condition, as possible. Conservation, though it touches preservation on the one side, reaches out towards redevelopment through the sympathetic improvement and enhancement of the existing architectural, historic or natural features which distinguish the buildings or area to be conserved. Most of the buildings in this book were sufficiently important to merit preservation rather than conservation, but in the terms of London's future, conservation in its widest sense must be the objective, and preservation of historic buildings must be seen as part of it.

London is threatened with the grim prospect of a Manhattan-like future, of becoming a city of the very rich and the very poor, a city unattainable and increasingly unattractive to the middle classes and to the younger families with children to bring up. This is being brought nearer by the extensive redevelopment of the central area, first for offices, and now for hotels. This is a redevelopment which local authorities are reluctant to veto because of its beneficial effect on economic growth and indeed on the income from rates, though indirectly, by decreasing the area available for housing, it exacerbates the local housing shortage and the strain on the commuting transport services.

The retention of key historic buildings – and indeed whole areas of older dwellings properly rehabilitated – can do a great deal to keep Central London human in scale and therefore still attractive to residents. With the increasing saturation of our commuting transport and our dormitory areas, this should be a primary aim, and one of the most important practical ways in which we can benefit from our remaining historical buildings.

It is encouraging that we are moving towards a more flexible town-planning policy where piecemeal redevelopment is more acceptable, and this may help to bridge the historic gap between the adherents of 'preservation' and 'progress', both shorthand terms for wide spectra of opinion and political creeds.

The other arguments for retaining historic buildings, even in the face of modern economic pressures, are really two – the value of the building itself as a work of art, and the psychological effect on people of too much demolition and redevelopment, a reason being given increasing recognition by town-planning theorists.

The great exponent of the antiquarian argument was William Morris, a founding father of the movement. His often quoted dictum summarises the arguments of the preservationist right:

> It has been most truly said that these old buildings do not belong to us only: that they belonged to our forefathers and they will belong to our descendants unless we play them false. They are

not in any sense our property, to do as we like with them. We are only trustees for those who come after us . . .

It is not difficult to imagine the horror with which such a statement was regarded in 1877, when property was truly a sacred interest, and the opposition to Sir John Lubbock's Ancient Monuments Bill in the years 1873–9 was an eloquent tribute to its economic and emotional strength. Today we accept a great deal more control in every aspect of our daily lives, and Morris's primarily antiquarian argument is probably less vulnerable to the counter-argument that the owner of a building has the right to destroy it for his private profit, than to the argument that society in general may benefit more from its demolition and redevelopment than from its retention.

The most fashionable form of 'public good' has varied from decade to decade. In 1932 the L.C.C. decided to rebuild old Waterloo Bridge in the interests of traffic; in 1961 the Conservative Government decided to endorse British Transport's contention that saving the Euston Arch was not worth £180,000; in 1966 Richard Crossman as Minister of Housing decided to demolish the Packington Estate because of the extra 120 homes that total rebuilding would give. Traffic, public money and homes for Londoners are still powerful enemies for any historic building, but we have, I believe – and hope – became more sophisticated in our vision of public benefit.

Once we accept that a building can be a work of art, then we can probably use the criteria laid down by the Waverley Committee in 1952 for forbidding the export of a work of art, for urging the retention of a historic building. These criteria were that it is closely associated with our history and national life, of outstanding aesthetic importance, or of outstanding significance for the study of some particular branch of art, learning or history. These principles are fairly widely accepted, though argument can and does take place on their application. Moreover while the motives for the refusal of an export licence can be narrowly chauvinistic, the retention of an important building does not only benefit the Londoner – or the Parisian or the Venetian – but it is the only way in which it can be preserved as part of the heritage of Western Europe.

There is another major reason for retaining buildings – because they provide the easiest and most direct way of understanding the past. The Gowers Committee, set up in 1948 by Sir Stafford Cripps to report on 'houses of historical importance', saw this as a reason for spending public money on them at a time of stringent national economy and in the face of demands of post-war urban reconstruction. They concerned themselves largely with the greater country houses, partly from the (often mistaken) belief that important town houses would be safe 'under the eye of the local authorities', but their arguments cover the safeguarding of such urban houses. They, too, 'constitute a national asset whose loss would be irrevocable' as the Pilgrim Trust said of country houses, they too 'mirror . . . our social history and domestic life'. In an even wider sense the historic *quartiers* of our towns demonstrate

> . . . in planning, design and construction . . . in ordered un-broken sequence, how the English home [and the English city] was adapted to changing conditions, social, economic, political and technical, as well as to fresh aesthetic ideals and a new intellectual outlook.

Some of this living history can still be saved – even in London, where its preservation is yet more difficult than in historic provincial towns.

A newly recognised motive for retaining older buildings is the disorientation caused to people by the total destruction of their environment. Modern redevelopment is particularly guilty of this – every neighbourhood in London can show instances of schemes which ignore the original street plan of the area, and substitute the inhuman scale of high-rise flats or a new office block for four- and five-storey traditional terrace houses. Even the fashionable palliative public open space is a poor substitute for private front and back gardens. There are many administrative faults in this sort of redevelopment which make the situation worse, such as the scale on which it is carried out, and the shifting of whole neighbourhood populations hither and thither to suit the availability of new Council developments, and the substitution of the High Street multiple shops for the smaller private trader who cannot afford to take premises in new developments. The definite dislike of high-rise housing amongst the people who actually have to live there contributes to the dislike of 'being redeveloped', and, together with the feeling of rootlessness and being at the mercy of an impersonal Council, has probably done as much as anything to engender the interest in conservation and the wider aspects of amenity which has been such a feature of post-war England.

The instability and unhappiness created by such wholesale redevelopment is gradually being recognised by town-planners and sociologists. This is leading to a more flexible attitude to redevelopment and greater sympathy for older buildings amongst town-planners, who in the immediate post-war period had little time for the preservation of historic buildings.

The movement towards redevelopment in equally dense but more popular traditional terrace housing makes it much easier to save the odd historic building or even the occasional group, which becomes an enhancement rather than merely an impediment.

Finally there is the economic argument – the tourist attraction of London's older streets and more interesting buildings. This is now a serious consideration in a decade when London tourist visitors have risen from one million in 1960 to 6½ million in 1970, and a figure of 12–15 million tourists has been forecast for 1980.

## The Battle for Preservation

The fight to save historic buildings in London runs parallel to – and in some praiseworthy instances rather ahead of – that of the rest of the country. Because of the greater land values, redevelopment in London has been more frequent and more lucrative with greater resulting losses of early buildings. On the other hand, once the desirability of preservation was established, its greater size and wealth enabled the London County Council to spend more freely on its historic buildings.

Legislation for the preservation of historic buildings starts, in London as elsewhere, with the Ancient Monuments Act in 1882. This listed twenty-nine early monuments, of which the most important was Stonehenge, the ownership or guardianship of which was to be vested in the Commissioner of Works, and for whose future upkeep the Government would be responsible. It was hardly relevant to densely populated London as the term 'ancient monument' expressly excluded any inhabited dwelling house. It did, however, establish the idea of maintaining such monuments with public money, and brought England into line with other European countries like France, Italy and Denmark, who already had varying degrees of government protection for ancient monuments and historic buildings.

A number of campaigns to save important buildings did occur in the 1870s and 1880s, mostly skirmishes in the pages of *The Times*, in local or Parliamentary committees, or in the courts, intended to make the vandal bow before the threat of public odium. Occasionally, as in some of the fights for the City churches, these were successful, but most of them were tragically ineffective.

In 1893 two significant events occurred in London. One was the acquisition by the L.C.C. of the York Watergate in the Embankment Gardens under the London Open Spaces Act, in order to preserve it. The other was the demolition, also by the L.C.C., of two important buildings in Bromley-by-Bow, one of which was a former royal palace (see page 24). These were purchased by the London School Board who, unaware of their importance, demolished them for a new school. This unhappy event crystallised the private opposition to demolition in London which had been growing since the 1870s.

This opposition was primarily antiquarian and architectural in flavour, and concerned not so much with the impossible struggle to save, as with the necessity to record. The first step was the formation of the Society for Photographing Relics of Old London, because of the threat to the Oxford Arms in 1875 (see page 194). The 120 photographs they issued between 1875 and 1886 mostly record seventeenth-century houses and inns, nearly all of which vanished before 1900. The National Society for the Protection of Ancient Buildings was founded by William Morris in 1877. This society was originally more concerned with the vandalism of restorers than that of demolishers, a 'better dead than red' attitude which was modified in the light of practical experience.

In 1893, however, the London Survey Committee was privately formed to record important buildings so that at least no more unintentional vandalism should occur. Under the editorship of C. R. Ashbee the first volume, significantly dealing with Bromley-by-Bow, was published in 1900. This record of a single parish in the outer suburbs is important enough as the prototype for the forty volumes of *The Survey of London* but it also contains an introduction in which Ashbee set out the arguments for conservation and the preservation of historic buildings and also of amenity in the widest sense. He was particularly concerned for the intelligent development of the outer suburbs, then being exploited by private speculators for cheap housing. The older mansions with their historic parks were peculiarly vulnerable:

> Nothing is done to protect the open spaces, the trees or gardens, that might with proper planning be preserved; if there is any beautiful object of the past, some house, perhaps, that could be utilised for library, club, museum, school or parish purposes, it is torn down and sold to the wreckers for its value in old materials. . . .

There was also a plea for the establishment of 'small municipal museums in different parts of London, connected in one way or another with local organisations and, wherever possible, set in some historic house and surrounded by the garden that is already in existence'. He claimed that such a museum could have been established in Bromley-by-Bow, housed in the old palace itself and making an important cultural neighbour for the new school.

The breadth of vision of the Survey Committee was extremely important for the future. It was a movement away from narrow antiquarianism towards a utilitarianism much more broadly based in its appeal, and indispensable if the importance of preservation was to be recognised in the more democratic period which lay ahead. The *Survey* was seen as an essential preliminary to better planning for the more profitable use of all London's amenities by her citizens. The L.C.C. endorsed this by going into partnership with the Survey Committee for the publication of its volumes, a partnership which continued until 1953, when the Council took sole responsibility.

In 1898, the L.C.C. obtained authority to purchase or to contribute towards expenditure on the 'preservation of buildings and places of architectural or historical interest'. This formula is very familiar today, but at the time it was farsighted in the powers that it gave the Council, and in its recognition of the importance of 'buildings' as opposed to 'ancient monuments'. The first use they made of their powers was to buy 17 Fleet Street, one of the finest half-timbered buildings left in London. An even more hopeful indication for the future was the way in which the new Kingsway scheme was planned to preserve the two Strand churches, in marked contrast to the routing of Northumberland Avenue twenty years before (see page 20).

The Edwardian era was an important time for the growth of interest in preservation. There was a large educated middle class, with the time, energy and knowledge to make a fuss and the money to support public subscription funds. At the same time excellent workmanship could still be obtained relatively cheaply. London, as the centre of not only the country but of the British Empire, had the means and the responsibility to preserve its past.

Despite this, the threats to historic buildings continued both from private developers and indeed from those same Americans who were buying both pictures and parts of buildings for shipment to the United States.

In 1911 the threat to Tattersall Castle in Lincolnshire, parts of which were to be ripped out, so aroused public opinion that the Ancient Monuments Consolidation and Amendment Act was put on the statute book. This was the first really comprehensive legislation on the subject, and established the principle that a building remaining in private ownership, and not maintained by the State, could none the less be put on the list of ancient monuments, and could be regarded in some sense as public property. The only buildings excluded from the provisions of the Act were inhabited dwelling-houses, or ecclesiastical buildings in ecclesiastical use. A list of buildings throughout the country was to be prepared, and owners were to be informed accordingly. Once informed, they had to give one month's notice of any intention to alter or demolish. The Commissioners could then make a preservation order on the building, valid only for eighteen months unless confirmed by Parliament.

The new measure was warmly welcomed, particularly so because of the plight of 75 Dean Street, Soho, an early Georgian house, recently restored, whose owner could find no purchaser or tenant. The first order under the new Act was made on this house in January 1914, and a month later the Commissioner of Works introduced a Bill to confirm it. The fate of this Bill revealed the real weakness of the Act, and it is significant that only two other, non-controversial Preservation Orders were made under it. It made no provision for financial aid to the owner of a building subject to an Order, thus imposing a heavy burden which seemed grossly inequitable to public opinion at the time. The House of Lords Select Committee upheld the owner's appeal against the order, and in due course the house was demolished (see page 27).

The inter-war years saw appalling losses among important West End houses, many of whose owners were faced with tempting offers from developers. The post-war slump and the depression meant that there was little public money for saving historic buildings, though on occasion the very rich stepped in and stumped up, as Lord Rothermere did for Bethlehem Hospital. It is arguable that Waterloo Bridge and the Adelphi Terrace, both of which required parliamentary sanction for their destruction, might have been saved in a period of greater affluence.

In 1924, the Government set up the Royal Fine Art Commission to advise it on matters of artistic importance generally, a wide field which covers the demolition of important historic buildings, and also the decision on what is to replace them. Reference is not mandatory, and a good deal of this work is done tactfully behind the scenes, though this has not prevented outspoken criticism on occasion. For this reason, its failures tend to be more publicised than its successes and a distorted picture is given of its effectiveness. None the less, the past history of some controversies drive one to ask why the Government maintains the Commission and disregards its advice.

There were important legislative changes in the 1930s, less effective than they might have been because of the state of public finances, but encouraging pointers for the future. The first of these was the Ancient Monuments Act of 1931, which extended the period of notice required for demolition, and also the period during which a Preservation Order was effective. The Historic Buildings and Ancient Monuments Act of 1933 simplified the procedure, and also allowed for the payment of compensation to an owner or occupier suffering loss from such an order.

For London, the Town and Country Planning Act of 1932 was more significant. Under this, local authorities were given the right to make Preservation Orders on buildings they considered important. Again this Act foundered for lack of money. In 1935, Norfolk House, possibly the most important great mansion still standing in London, was threatened with demolition for redevelopment. Under its newly acquired powers the L.C.C. could have saved it – but they could not afford to compensate the developer. One important consequence of the Act was that the L.C.C., already playing an increasing role in the *Survey*, with a responsibility for photographing and measuring unavoidable losses, undertook the listing of important buildings in London, so that it would be in a position to intervene in an emergency.

The losses between the wars were chiefly among eighteenth-century buildings, and the casualties among Adam houses, particularly the Adelphi (see page 96), and the threat to the City churches provoked a reaction which led to the formation in 1937 of the Georgian Group of the S.P.A.B., specifically devoted to the study and preservation of what were then regarded almost as modern buildings. The group's first great battle was for Abingdon Street, Westminster, a highly organised, much publicised and successful campaign, whose results were sadly nullified by the war (see pages 92–3).

With the Second World War came other devastating losses, either in the Blitz or because of what may be termed 'sympathetic demolition', but there were also great opportunities for reform and reconstruction of the planning machinery. Two minor innovations occurred during the war itself. In 1940, the National Buildings Record was set up, under the indefatigable Walter Godfrey, to try and list and record as much as possible before it was destroyed. This has given us a vital record of pre-war and post-war London, and the National Monuments Record, as it now is, is an integral part of the Ministry's listing machinery. Under the Town and Country Planning Act of 1944, the newly appointed Minister of Town and Country Planning was empowered to set up machinery for listing historic buildings. This Act acknowledged for the first time the real importance of the occupied dwelling-house, a category which had been effectively excluded under all the Ancient Monuments Acts.

The listing procedure was more fully set out in the 1947 Town and Country Planning Act, under which the investigators of the Ministry have been gradually recording historic buildings throughout the country. Buildings are listed Grade I, Grade II*, Grade II and Grade III. On the first three categories there are fairly strict provisions. Grade I buildings, of which there are about 3,500 in the whole country, and 680 in London, are of such importance that under no circumstances should they be pulled down. Grade II required a really good reason for their destruction, or alteration to their exteriors, and in the case of Grade II*, interior alterations require consent. Grade III buildings had virtually no protection except that the owners had to give notice of intention to demolish. London, with about 20,000 listed buildings in 1970, contains about one-sixth of the country's listed buildings.

There were various flaws in the system, the results of which appear in this book. Primarily, the listing was very slow, much slower still outside London, and not always faultless, partly because the department was under-staffed, and partly because of the terms of reference. These were to list almost everything before 1700 (except for ancient monuments which were dealt with by a different set of experts in a totally separate Ministry), important buildings of 1700–1830, and to ignore almost everything built since. Thus extraordinary omissions occurred, such as the City of London Club and Londonderry House, though the L.C.C. did save a number of Victorian buildings by well-timed Preservation Orders.

Certain classes of building, though included in the lists, had no legal protection because their owners were exempt from control. The most notorious instances were the churches of all denominations which continued to enjoy their traditional freedom from control not only for churches but also for clergy dwellings or church schools, and the 'Crown', a wide umbrella covering all Ministries, such departments as the Post Office, even as lessees of a building, and the Crown Estate Commissioners, who are important West End landlords.

Another weakness of the 1947 Act lay in its powers to enforce its provisions. It was, however, probably flouted less grossly in London than elsewhere, though flagrant demolitions of listed buildings have occurred in the outer London boroughs. Under the Act, an owner could always plead that the building was beyond restoration, and there was little compulsion on an unwilling owner to prevent decay. Even if an important building in good order was deliberately destroyed the maximum penalty was £100.

Without going to the lengths of hiring a bulldozer or introducing dry rot, the owner had a sporting chance of achieving demolition, since the onus was on the local authority to take action to prevent demolition or alteration. Thus under what has been called the 'sick typist' loophole, if the local authority failed to react to his notice of intention to demolish or alter by serving a Preservation Order, he could go ahead. Also the provisions for compensation in the event of a successful appeal against the Order were such to frighten off even the wealthy L.C.C. Even if he lost the appeal, the owner could claim that the preserved building was incapable of 'beneficial use', a serious and expensive consideration for a specialized building, or one left high and dry in an area whose character had entirely altered. If this claim could be substantiated then he could serve a purchase notice, leaving the L.C.C. not only with a large capital outlay but running costs also. The Council suffered only one purchase order under the Act, but there were a number of other occasions on which it was inhibited from effective action by the danger of incurring such a notice.

The 1947 Act was an undoubted improvement, but its limitations were severe, as the Gowers Committee pointed out:

> Taken as a whole, the powers of negative preservation are imposing on paper, but in practice they have proved ineffective owing to the delay in putting them into operation and the undue reliance they place upon Authorities heavily burdened with other duties. . . . Nor are the financial provisions such as to encourage local authorities to exercise their powers. . . . Any powers of positive preservation the law purports to provide are useless for saving 'inhabited' houses.

The Report of 1950 highlighted the position of historic buildings which were expensive to maintain, largely the problem of the great country houses, and led to a number of reforms which benefited London as well. In 1953 the Historic Buildings Council was set up with a Treasury grant to aid the owners of historic buildings in dire need, a very much cheaper alternative for the nation than taking them over. In 1962, the Local Authorities (Historic Buildings) Act was passed to allow local authorities to give grants to the owners of historic buildings of local rather than national importance.

The growth of local amenity societies and other voluntary bodies was one of the important features of the 1950s and 1960s. In 1958, the Victorian Society joined the S.P.A.B. and the Georgian Group to form an increasingly formidable trinity of architectural societies, ready to do battle for almost any building of merit, however modern.

The formation of the Civic Trust in 1957 was even more of a landmark. In some ways it is, as its name suggests, the urban counterpart of the National Trust (founded in 1895), but it has a federal structure based on the local amenity societies and pressure groups present in ever larger numbers since 1945. It repudiates any accusation of controlling its member societies and sees its role as encouragement and information rather than direction. There are, of course, a number of older societies in the London area, notably the London Society itself, founded in 1912, but what is new about the amenity groups of the 1960s is the very much wider social spectrum they represent, indicating a much more generally accepted interest in local amenity, a term which covers a great deal more than historic buildings.

## The Situation Today

In 1967 and 1968, two important new Acts were passed which embodied most of the criticisms of the existing legislation.

The importance of the Civic Trust was shown when the Civic Amenities Act of 1967 was introduced as a private member's Bill by Duncan Sandys, President of the Trust, and not as a government measure. It is one of the most influential acts to reach the statute book in this way.

The Act's preamble was significant: it was designed to 'make further provision for the protection and improvement of buildings of architectural or historic interest and of the character of such areas . . .' This was the first time that statutory recognition was given to the value of a group of buildings, individually less important than as members of that group, and also the first time that any attempt was made to define and preserve the atmosphere of an area, something which can be lost as easily through an unsympathetic restoration as through demolition. It was also another dynamic step towards rehabilitation and discreet renovation. Under it the local authorities have the right and duty to designate Conservation Areas 'the character or appearance of which it is desirable to preserve or enhance'. In support they can make loans as well as grants, and can take various other steps from exemplary repairs to their own buildings in such areas, to the sympathetic relaxation of building regulations, the making of improvement grants under the Housing Acts, measures for traffic relief, and a use of Building Preservation Orders (now Notices) to supplement inadequate historic building lists. In London, the designation of such areas is done by the Cities of London and Westminster and the London Boroughs, advised by the G.L.C. Historic Buildings Division, and in many cases urged on by their local amenity societies, whose existence is now officially recognised.

Major problems are presented by the preservation of buildings or the conservation of areas at either end of the financial scale. It takes a remarkably tough Council to stand up to a developer with a well-briefed architect who wishes to redevelop an expensive and important site, because the arguments on the side of change are exceedingly persuasive. For instance they are turning down a large increase in the rateable value of the area and face the very real danger of stagnation, if no one else is ready to put the money up for conservation and renewal rather than total redevelopment.

Attractive fringe benefits like the rerouting of roads and off-street carparks can also accrue from a large redevelopment scheme.

In areas of low property values other problems are presented since the owners who will buy and modernise workmen's cottages in Kensington are not attracted to houses of greater architectural importance in less fashionable neighbourhoods. In these the local authorities are faced with having to modernise houses themselves to rehouse their own tenants, possibly, but not inevitably, at a lower density than they could achieve by demolition and building blocks of flats. In between, however, lie a large number of areas where rehabilitation is not only desirable but economically possible, like Paddington, where the G.L.C. is renovating a large area. Despite minor defects the idea of a conservation area is a major step forward, though public pressure is now building up for more effective control over non-listed buildings in conservation areas. The Civic Amenities Act also plugged a few other loopholes in the protection of historic buildings.

The following year, the Labour Government brought in another Town and Country Planning Act. This increased the penalties for the wilful destruction of a historic building to a fine of £250 or three months' imprisonment on summary conviction, and for conviction on indictment twelve months' imprisonment or an unlimited fine which should be related to the likely profit reaped by the offender.

It also strengthened the protection for historic buildings in Grades I and II. Demolition or alteration now had to have positive consent from the local authority. Proposed demolitions or alterations had to be advertised, and the Minister and six national bodies – the three architectural societies, the Royal Commission on Historic Monuments, The British Council for Archaeology and the Ancient Monuments Society – all had to be informed.

There are further powers by which a local authority can serve a repair notice on a recalcitrant or neglectful owner, backed up by the ultimate sanction of compulsory purchase. If a listed building is deliberately allowed to decay to facilitate redevelopment, as happened to tens, if not hundreds, of buildings between 1947 and 1968, the local authority can purchase the building or even the site, and only 'minimum compensation' will be paid, on terms which disregard any development potential the site might have.

These provisions are strengthened by the Ministry's circular to local authorities, for the importance of legislation lies largely in the spirit in which it is administered. 'The presumption should be in favour of preservation except where a strong case can be made out for a grant of consent [for demolition or alteration] after application of the criteria mentioned.' The importance of preserving listed buildings and designating conservation areas is accepted fairly widely by the G.L.C. and the London Boroughs. This change in public opinion is being reinforced by the revision of the Ministry's lists of historic buildings, both by the inclusion of buildings inexplicably missed out of the original lists, and by the addition of later buildings. The search for profitable sites for redevelopment in London is already endangering some pre-war buildings, and it is arguable that the Ministry's investigators should be more adventurous and list still more recent buildings, already in need of protection, so that the sad story of our Victorian buildings is not repeated.

In London, the G.L.C. maintains its own Historic Buildings Division responsible for making additions to the lists, for advising the Historic Buildings Board, the G.L.C.'s elected committee, and other G.L.C. bodies, for administering the grants system, for bringing out the Survey of London, and for putting up the famous blue plaques on the houses of the famous. On all this out of a total London budget of over £200 million in 1970–1, £165,000 was spent on the running of the division, £110,000 on the running of the Council's own properties like Kenwood, £27,000 on the *Survey*, and grants of £20,000 were made to the owners of historic buildings. Although this last figure is to be raised this year to £25,000 it is still only a pound for every one of London's listed properties. More significantly it is only a tiny fraction of the golden harvest derived from visitors to London.

Although legislation has improved the situation enormously, we must not be lulled into a Panglossian view of the future of our remaining historic buildings. The question marks that hang over them are really two: do they command a sufficiently high priority in public opinion? and if so, are there adequate legislative and administrative safeguards to protect them from stupid or malicious destruction?

The answer to the second question is probably yes: provided the building is listed and the local authority is interested in and aware of what is happening to its historic buildings. There are suggestions that stricter aesthetic control is needed over the architectural details of listed buildings. This need may well become more pressing as the effects of the Leasehold Reform Act of 1967, which destroyed the traditional tight control of the great estates over large parts of Inner London, become more obvious. Under certain circumstances there are provisions for a local planning authority to exercise the sort of strict management over the maintenance and appearance of historic areas formerly exercised by estate surveyors, and this may be necessary to maintain the external uniformity of details and colour which is part of the charm of a Regency terrace.

However, the basic threats remain, as the list of important buildings which are now threatened shows (see Section VIII). Ignorance and public indifference may have diminished, but the needs of urban renewal, for more housing, for more offices and more hotels, for more efficient roads, for new patterns of public transport, all remain, to be balanced against the need and the advisability of preserving what is left of London's historic and architectural past. In essence, however, the matter depends on how much society is prepared to spend not only in the crudest sense, but in the allocation of resources of time and skill, both publicly and privately, to schemes that will preserve rather than destroy. This is already happening with some public authority urban renewal, and there are encouraging signs that private developers too can see the benefits, in every sense, of restoring older buildings.

A great deal can be done by intelligent planning, by taking the need to preserve historic buildings into consideration in the earliest stages. Tragically often in the immediate post-war years, outline planning permission was given which involved the demolition of listed buildings. By the time the danger was realised it was too late to withdraw or modify permission without incurring claims for heavy compensation.

It can be shown that certain buildings were lost because of the peculiar greed of a private developer, or because of the insistence by some learned institution that the needs of its members overrode any normal consideration of amenity, or because some great estate saw the preservation of a small group of buildings as an obstacle to a cherished and lucrative master-plan, but in all these cases the buildings could have been saved by firmer planning control. If the directive to civil servants and local officials by their elected masters had been stronger, the presence of a historic building in an area scheduled for alteration or demolition would have been taken really seriously, not only by the experts and the amateur pressure groups, but by the members of town-planning committees at metropolitan and borough levels, and by the architects and their clients, whether local authorities or private developers.

The preservation of our historic buildings is no mean undertaking and of importance to future generations, for it is our children and grandchildren who will enjoy the environment we have created for them. They may well reproach us for our negligence, as we find inexplicable the motives of the previous generations who destroyed the buildings shown in this book.

# I
# MANSIONS

'If we sought for a particular feature distinguishing London from the other capitals of Europe, apart from its immense proportions, it would probably be found in the number of its large houses, many of which are indeed the private palaces that I have here called them . . . its great houses are, as they have always been, a distinctive note in the picture, and *mutatis mutandis*, may in many cases compare with those palaces for which Venice was once famous. But there is this difference . . . the latter have in most instances passed from their once high estate to more utilitarian uses, and their chief glory lies in the beauty of their exteriors: whereas, if the majority of the London palaces cannot lay claim to such outwardly striking attributes, nearly every one contains . . . a wealth of beautiful objects.'

Though E. Beresford Chancellor wrote this only sixty years ago, such complacency seems astonishing today when only six of his fifteen 'private palaces' still stand. The interiors of many have been turned into offices, while none of them, of course, now contain the art treasures he described. A number of the other important houses he mentions, which were then already government offices or had suffered other utilitarian fates, have also disappeared.

In 1870, the palaces of London still lay scattered between the City and the West End as the *drang nach Westen* had placed them. In the City itself were the few remaining mansions of the leading citizens, less fashionable than those of the Stuart courtiers, rebuilt substantially in the late seventeenth century after the Fire of London. In Bloomsbury and stretching along the Strand were the houses of the courtiers, who after the Fire ceased to build within the walls. St James's Square and Whitehall came into their own in 1700, benefiting both from the proximity of the Court, and of St James's Park. Mayfair gained fashionable favour in the mid-eighteenth century, and despite the later attractions of Belgravia, remained the place to live, until the aristocracy ceased to live in palaces at all.

There were also a number of suburban houses, originally built outside metropolitan London, but which have gradually been absorbed by the tide of bricks and mortar. Occasionally these houses survived, like Canonbury Tower, or even Holland House – destroyed not by economic trends but by enemy action – but many more, like the manor house at Battersea, have fallen on evil days and finally been pulled down in a ruinous condition. A comment on a house in St James's Square, will serve for many:

'Such relics of old London are, however, foredoomed to destruction so soon as their owners neglect to keep them in reasonable repair; and in the case of Cleveland House the intrinsic value of the site was too great to permit the retention of such a mouldering vestige of antiquity.'

The last hundred years has seen an accelerated destruction of palaces, mansions and also, indeed, the houses of the richer members of the middle class – important both artistically and as a sociological record. To a greater degree than any other single class of building they have been destroyed, leaving London with fewer important noblemen's houses than any capital city in Western Europe with comparable wealth and history. The reasons for this loss are many. Besides the obvious fact that taxation has made the large London house an impossibility even for the rich, the increasing specialisation of modern building has made conversion unattractive and relatively expensive. At the same time the size and height of modern buildings makes necessary the comprehensive redevelopment of large sites with high density, and involves site works to a considerable depth, which can damage older neighbours – as St Paul's Cathedral has been damaged.

Though the older City mansions were already causing concern to antiquarians a century ago, there was then no such anxiety about the future of houses in fashionable areas still lived in by the very rich. Such houses, however, became peculiarly vulnerable in the 1920s and 1930s. In the words of a German journalist, who blamed the leasehold system for making it difficult for a contractor to acquire a large enough site for redevelopment:

'This explains why contractors . . . swoop down on the few remaining historical town mansions of the aristocracy to demolish them and build blocks of palatial flats on the sites, because they cannot buy the requisite number of modest terrace houses. This, of course, mars the beauty of the city, which is fast losing the few typical aristocratic houses it once possessed. . . .'

By 1931, when this was written, many of the important houses had already disappeared. Though after the war they were given statutory protection by the Planning Acts, this has not prevented the disappearance of Londonderry and Bath Houses.

Many of those that remain have suffered a remodelling inside that must destroy much of their interest, for sociologists as for architectural historians, or indeed for those of us who crowd with enthusiasm to Woburn or Longleat. It is impossible to argue in favour of inequality of wealth merely so that the interiors and exteriors of great London houses can be maintained intact, but it is not so bizarre to argue that, in this age of folk museums, it is scandalous that no government agency has thought to preserve and maintain any single one of the great London houses as they might have been in their heyday. How fascinating to see not only ballroom, withdrawing-room and library, but bedrooms, dressing rooms, Servants' Hall – as strictly regimented and socially conscious as any hat-racked and carpeted government office – kitchen and scullery, 'above-stairs' and 'below-stairs', connected by row upon row of bells.

Though of less individual importance, and less dramatic in their disappearance, the medium-sized town houses, lived in by the upper-middle classes, have also suffered, either being demolished or converted into flats. Latterly, these have included a number of interesting houses built by such architects as Norman Shaw and Edwin Lutyens for the late Victorian and Edwardian new rich, houses as important in the history of architecture in England as Kent's Devonshire House or Robert Adam's Harewood House.

The needs of the 'medium-sized householder' in Mayfair and Belgravia were already being analysed in the late 1920s, in the light of the cinema and the motor car:

'. . . the needs supplied by the home are being satisfied from outside, the library substituted by the wireless, the dining-room and kitchen by the cheap amusing restaurant, the drawing-room by the garage . . . the home therefore, has ceased to be a background and a setting, and has shrunk to being once more a shelter.'

This shelter could indeed be provided much more efficiently by a block of purpose-built flats than by conversion, and logically, and indeed correctly in the light of need for urban renewal, the policies of the larger and better-run London estates took this trend into account, and built accordingly, 'The Grosvenor House of the Dukes of Westminster is replaced by the Grosvenor House of innumerable misters.'

## NORTHUMBERLAND HOUSE

Northumberland House was the last of a line of noblemen's palaces which stretched along the Strand in the seventeenth century. It was built in 1605 by Henry Howard, Earl of Northampton, to the designs of Bernard Jansen and Gerard Christmas, on the site of a pre-Reformation convent. It passed into the possession of the Percy family in 1642, and was known as Northumberland House until its demolition in 1874, for the making of Northumberland Avenue to connect Trafalgar Square with the newly made Embankment. This is the earliest known view of the House from the river, by Hollar, showing the turrets, two of which were removed in 1759, and those on the street front being considerably lowered in 1780.

Since the Duke of Northumberland 'took a high and just view of the duties of his position in declining absolutely to frustrate the design' for Northumberland Avenue, the house was doomed and in July 1874, demolition began with the removal of the Percy lion to Syon House.

NORTHUMBERLAND HOUSE from Trafalgar Square in 1845, an early photograph by Fox-Talbot. 'The march of fashion westward had left it isolated amidst an uncongenial neighbourhood of small shops. . . . Commerce had overtaken it and overwhelmed it . . . with the Thames Embankment on one side and Trafalgar Square on the other. . . . Northumberland House was a standing anachronism, if not an impediment, which was designed to succumb to the influence of time and the Metropolitan Board of Works.' (Contemporary comment in the *Standard*.)

Unfortunately no photographs of the magnificent interiors were taken before demolition. The Duke of Northumberland preserved the Adam decorations to the drawing-room and ballroom, but not those of the Picture Gallery designed by Roger Morris in 1749, shown here in a drawing from the *Illustrated London News* of 1874

## HOLLAND HOUSE, 1925

Holland House, the only other Jacobean mansion in London to survive into modern times, was built in 1607 by John Thorpe for Sir Walter Cope, who became the father-in-law of the first Earl of Holland. Not only was it an important house of the period, one of the models which rekindled the interest of Victorian architects in the Jacobean style, but it was best known as the centre of Whig wit and learning, under the third Lord Holland, nephew of the great Whig statesman, Charles James Fox. In the words of the greatest of Whig historians:

'In what language shall we speak of that house, once celebrated for its rare attractions to the furthest ends of the civilised world . . .? Yet a few years, and the shades and structures may follow their illustrious masters. The wonderful city which, ancient and gigantic as it is, continues to grow as fast as a young town of logwood . . . in Michigan, may soon displace those turrets and gardens which are associated with so much that is interesting and noble. . . . The time is coming when, perhaps, a few old men, the last survivors of our generation, will in vain seek, amidst new streets, and squares, and railway stations, for the site of that dwelling which was in their youth the favourite resort of wits and beauties, of painters and poets, of scholars, philosophers, and statesmen. They will then remember . . . many objects once familiar to them, the avenue and terrace, the busts and the paintings, the carving, the grotesque gilding, the enigmatic mottoes . . .'

Lord Macaulay was rightly pessimistic: though the house survived the danger of redevelopment until 1939, it was badly damaged by bombing in September 1941. The ruins of the house and the gardens are now a public park.

# Seventeenth-century Houses

A surprisingly large number of important City merchant's houses, some pre-Fire, but mostly of the late seventeenth century, survived into the latter half of the nineteenth century. They were carefully recorded by devoted City historians because it was generally recognized that they could not expect to survive. Some were demolished for various reasons – for road widening, for railway extensions or in the course of commercial redevelopment, always vulnerable because cheaper than more modern premises – and some were 'improved out of existence', in the words of one irate antiquarian.

In some cases, such as Crosby Hall, moved to Chelsea Embankment in 1909–10, and Sir Paul Pindar's House, some relics of which ended up at the Victoria and Albert Museum, parts of these important old buildings were preserved. The information that a ceiling or a staircase would go to South Kensington was often accepted too easily as a consolation for the loss of an historic building – it is the substitution of a stuffed head or paw for the living animal, but better than the deliberate total destruction since 1945 of some important and salvageable buildings.

The chief value of these houses, besides their historical connections, was in their fine carved or brick fronts, sometimes pilastered as in Nos 8 and 9 Great St Helen's, and in their magnificent carved staircases, fireplaces and panelling, and elaborate plaster ceilings, such as that in a house in St Botolph Lane. The grander houses disappeared first, partly because they often stood in a private court; many minor houses survived in street frontages for longer, often radically refronted and completely remodelled inside.

THE OLD PALACE at Bromley-by-Bow was traditionally associated with James I, and by some authorities attributed to the architect John Thorpe. Its demolition – of 'the finest building in East London' – by the L.C.C. School Board in 1893 aroused much public indignation and became one of the *causes célèbres* of the preservation movement. C. R. Ashbee pointed out that 'We now have on the site of King James' Palace a well-built Board School . . . sanitary, solid, grey, grim, and commonplace. What we might have had with a little thought, and with no extra expense . . . would have been an ideal Board School with a record of every period of English history from the time of Henry VIII, as a daily object lesson for the little citizens of Bromley, a school-house that contained panelling of James I, carving of William III, the modelled plaster-work . . . of the early Jacobean time, rooms all the more gracious for the sumptuous additions of the later Stuarts . . . a school house to be proud of . . .'

The east front looking on to St Leonard's Street, showing the division into two merchant's houses made about 1750. The mullioned windows had then been replaced with sliding sashes. The pyramidal towers at either end of the façade were originally higher, but were cut down. Though one of the finest surviving suburban Jacobean buildings, it was not unique, and a large number of other manor-houses in outer London disappeared during the same period.

## SIR PAUL PINDAR'S HOUSE

Sir Paul Pindar's house, Bishopsgate Street in 1812, built in the reign of James I, and demolished in 1890 by the Great Eastern Railway. It was turned into a tavern in the eighteenth century. The carved oak frontage was taken to the Victoria and Albert Museum. Such wooden fronts were a fire hazard, and were forbidden by the Building Acts passed after the Great Fire.

CARLISLE HOUSE, Soho Square, *c.* 1938, is 'one of the most valuable survivals of old Soho', which like the City contained a number of mansions, belonging to courtiers and merchants. The house was not, as its name implies and tradition relates, built for Lord Carlisle, but upon speculation about 1685, and only became the residence of Lady Carlisle in 1718. At the end of the eighteenth century it was the establishment of Domenico Angelo, riding and fencing master to the young George III. It was then subdivided, and became a private hotel in 1860 and an antique furniture warehouse from 1873. It was the headquarters of the British Board of Film Censors when it was destroyed by bombing on 11 May 1940.

No. 10, on the south side of Nevill's Court, off Fetter Lane, a handsome seventeenth-century house which survived until 1906 as the mission house of the Moravian brethren in England.

No. 75 Dean Street was one of a group of four houses built by the carpenter, Thomas Richmond, about 1733, and therefore not strictly a detached mansion. It had, however, a well-known painted staircase and some finely decorated rooms, important enough to find a home in an American museum when the house was demolished.

The paintings were widely but incorrectly attributed to Sir James Thornhill, or to his son-in-law, William Hogarth. This led to the house being the subject of the first, and tragically abortive, attempt to preserve a building under the Ancient Monuments Act of 1913. Despite the good intentions of the owner, who had spent £4000 on having the paintings restored in 1912, it was impossible to find an occupant. He planned to sell the house for demolition with provision for the best features to go to the Victoria and Albert Museum, a scheme vigorously opposed *inter alios* by *The Times*, who condemned the projected demolition as 'inexcusable vandalism'. On 16 January 1914, a preservation order was made by the First Commissioner of Works, warmly commended by *Country Life* for having made such 'timely use of his new powers'. The owner appealed against the preservation order, which made no provision for compensation of any sort, and the select committee of the House of Lords which heard the appeal in May 1914 allowed it, not so much because of the lack of merit of No. 75 Dean Street, as of the demerits of the Act.

Despite the offer of the owner to sell the house at cost to any authority ready to preserve it, no action was taken, the First World War intervened, and in 1919 the interior of the house including the paintings was dismantled by dealers who had bought them *in situ*.

The paintings proved impossible to salvage, but the staircase and ground-floor rooms were ultimately re-erected at the Art Institute of Chicago.

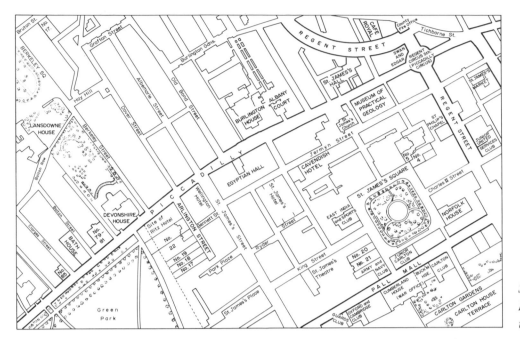

## The Palaces of The West End

A hundred years ago, western Piccadilly from Devonshire House to
Apsley House was 'elegant, expensive and aristocratic'. Despite the
intrusion of some clubs, and an early block of flats on the site of
Gloucester House, this *cachet* was retained until 1914. Since then
most of the old houses have been demolished and none, of course,
are in private hands. Amongst the casualties are No. 116, built by
Dusillon in 1848–51 for Henry Thomas Hope, the art collector and
banker, important as the first serious French building in London,
demolished in 1936; No. 85, latterly the Turf Club, but substantially
the mansion built about 1760 by Sir Robert Taylor for the Duke of
Grafton, and demolished in the early 1960s.

In 1925, Nos 79, 80 and 81 Piccadilly, together with No. 1 Stratton Street, famous as the home of the Baroness Burdett-Coutts, were demolished for the building of Stratton House.

DEVONSHIRE HOUSE was the most serious loss, both as William Kent's only surviving 'private palace' and, from the house's historical and political associations, as the focus of the opposition to George III, under the fifth Duke of Devonshire, and his beautiful wife, Georgiana.

Built in 1733 for the third Duke, the modesty of the house was not universally admired, and one contemporary compared it to an East India Company warehouse. This was less kind than Augustus Hare in 1878, who found it 'a perfectly unpretending building with a low-pillared entrance hall, [whose] winding marble staircase with wide shallow steps is admirably suited to the princely hospitalities of the Cavendishes.'

It was sold by the Duke in 1918, but was not redeveloped till 1924 for the erection of a block of flats on to the Park, and a hotel and offices behind on the long gardens which ran back to Lansdowne Passage.

Devonshire House, the Saloon in the 1890s, said to be the finest example extant of Kent's style. However austere the exterior the interior was magnificent. Part of it was remodelled by James Wyatt in 1811, and it was a fitting showcase for the Cavendish pictures, furniture and *objets d'art*.

## ARLINGTON STREET

Off Piccadilly, Arlington Street, Horace Walpole's 'Ministerial Street', could boast at least five important private houses in 1920. Three of these were demolished in 1934 for the erection of a block of flats; of the other two, one, No. 16, is a Club annexe, the other, No. 22, is an office.

With their 'fronts in the midst of the hurry and splendour of the town' and their 'backs in the quiet simplicity of the country', the houses on the western side were as agreeable and fashionable as any in London. Of the houses on the east side, four (Nos 11–12, 14–15) listed as grade III in 1950 have been demolished since, and Nos 4 and 5 look in a somewhat shabby condition.

No. 18 Arlington Street, whose last owner was Lord Faringdon, was a major loss, in national as well as London terms. 'Pomfret Castle', as it was known, was the only mid-eighteenth century Gothick house in London, and one of the very few major works by the talented amateur, Sanderson Miller (1717–80), whose Gothick buildings did much to set the stage for the taste, first for the picturesque, and later for the Gothic revival itself. It was built about 1760, with a gatehouse on to the street, behind which lay a private forecourt, and then the main block overlooking St James's Park.

Though the external ornament was rather shallow, the interior was covered with vigorous Gothic detailing, mostly inspired by Perpendicular originals.

The staircase was particularly fine, whole-hearted in its use of Gothic motives in a manner more reminiscent of 1860 than 1760.

So little was the Gothic revival regarded in 1934, that no effort was made to record the house in any detail by the L.C.C. or any other body, public or private, though we are fortunate that *Country Life* did take a series of photographs before demolition.

No. 19 Arlington Street was an early eighteenth-century town mansion, considerably altered by Adam for the Dundas family in 1763–6; it was described in 1921 as 'an interesting and almost untouched house remarkable as containing work of the earliest years of Robert Adam's career as an architect in London'. The entrance was still early Georgian in form, leading to the staircase entirely remodelled by Adam.

The Saloon on the first floor, redecorated by Adam, and with the
furniture designed by him for the room. The Boucher-Neilson
tapestries came from Moor Park, on which Adam also worked for
the Dundas family, and which was given up by them in 1784, when
the Arlington Street Saloon was refitted to take the tapestries.

BUCKINGHAM HOUSE, No. 91 Pall Mall, the staircase in 1907. Sir John Soane remodelled two early eighteenth-century houses for the first Marquess of Buckingham in 1792–5. The oval staircase with caryatides at either end shows Soane's genius for creating exciting spaces out of necessary apartments.

The house came on the market in 1847, when the second Duke of Buckingham was in financial difficulties, and found its way back into the hands of the Crown, who transferred it to the War Office. When the War Office moved to Whitehall it was demolished, some of the fittings being preserved for inclusion in the Whitehall building.

CUMBERLAND HOUSE, Pall Mall, built in 1761–7 for the Duke of York and subsequently occupied by his nephew, the Duke of Cumberland. The central block was designed by Matthew Brettingham, senior (1699–1769), and the wings were added, probably to an Adam design, in 1773 and 1809. Robert Adam also remodelled part of the interior in 1780–8.

Section through the house as designed by Brettingham.
The house was occupied from 1806 till 1906 by the War Office and its forerunner, the Ordnance Office. The western half was de-

molished in 1908 for the Royal Automobile Club, and the rest three years later for that Club's extension.

ST JAMES'S SQUARE preserved its appearance as a group of aristocratic mansions, if not all its social *cachet* as a desirable place to live, until 1930, since the clubs and other non-domestic users were housed either in converted mansions or in new buildings resembling houses rather than office blocks. The three sides of the square developed by the Earl of St Albans in the 1670s were remarkable for 'a high degree of uniformity and a remarkable lack of architectural elaboration', a uniformity later breached by rebuilding and alteration of the façades. Because of the wealth of the owners, a number of important architects were employed, including both Soane and Adam, making the losses in St James's Square the more serious. The development in the 1930s caused comment: 'What passes comprehension is that it should be possible for a square so famous and distinguished to be rebuilt in the way it is – piecemeal without regard to unity or continuity.' This was written about No. 21, built by R. B. Brettingham, with modifications by Soane, demolished together with its stableyard in July 1934, originally for a new National Sporting Club, to a design by Mewès and Davis. Then in 1935 the site was sold to the Distillers' Company, also employing Mewès and Davis, who produced a scheme by which Adam's façade for No. 20 was extended from three bays to seven. Whatever one may feel about Adam by the yard, it was a courteous attempt to conform, if to the letter rather than the spirit of the square, which has been completely abandoned in the case of the new Cleveland House and the two new club houses, the Junior Carlton and the Army and Navy. At the moment two of the most important houses, Nos 4 and 5, are virtually unoccupied. Their future use is in doubt and must be a matter for concern.

NORFOLK HOUSE in 1936, just before demolition. Built for the ninth Duke by Matthew Brettingham the elder in 1748–52, it was by far the most important house in the square despite its modest exterior, described by a contemporary writer as unworthy of the residence of the premier Duke of England.
It contained work of most periods of its two centuries of existence.

The drawing-rooms showing the ceiling after that by Kent at Holkham (in the nearer room). The nearer fireplace shows the influence of the French Rococo first seen in London here and at Chesterfield House.

The loss of Norfolk House was the more tragic, because it would have been possible for the London County Council to have saved the building under the newly passed Town and Country Planning Act of 1932. This was considered early in 1935, but rejected because of the heavy compensation which would have been payable.

The severely Palladian entrance hall with its marble floor, and its Doric entablature ornamented with the Norfolk badges.

PARK LANE. This panorama, recorded in 1927, shows not only
the villas – so curious because originally they were the backs of
houses in the more important Park Street – but also the Victorian
palaces which were inserted into gaps in the Georgian terraces. Not
only have most of these houses shown here disappeared, but Park
Lane, no longer retired and exclusive, has become the south-bound
carriage way of an urban motorway.

CAMELFORD HOUSE, at the top of Park Lane, was demolished about 1912. It was built by Lord Camelford, brother of William Pitt the Elder, for his own occupation. It was lived in for a short time by the ill-fated Princess Charlotte, daughter of the Prince Regent. Though very modest externally, it had splendid plasterwork and other interior decoration.

BROOKE HOUSE, built in 1870 by T. H. Wyatt (1807–80) for Sir Dudley Coutts Marjoribanks. The last owner was the millionaire Sir Ernest Cassell. The house was demolished in 1933.

Nos 27 and 28 Park Lane, which backed on to, and overlooked, the garden of Grosvenor House behind, which, though the London house of one of the greatest of English magnates, had the modest address of No. 33 Upper Grosvenor Street. Originally it was Gloucester House, after Henry, Duke of Gloucester, brother of George III. Despite a number of projects for total rebuilding, the first Marquess of Westminster moved into the house as it was in 1822. Thomas Cundy (1790–1867) built on the famous picture gallery (*overleaf*) and an entrance screen to the Upper Grosvenor Street entrance in 1843.

The Grosvenor Gallery in 1889.

Houses in Park Lane, immediately north of Aldford Street. 'At a time', wrote a contemporary, 'when everybody is rather startled by the rapidly changing appearance of Park Lane, and is loud in protests at the demolition of familiar houses, the responsibility of the landlord for the future must, in justice, be borne in mind.' He went on to point out that this replacement of houses for which it had become difficult to find tenants by flats was merely sound estate management.

Critics of the redevelopment of Park Lane in the 1930s must remember that a similar attitude in the 1790s gave us Bedford Square, and in the 1820s Bloomsbury and Belgravia. Is the real problem perhaps the inhumanity of scale of the modern block of flats or offices?

The same block in 1931, showing the change in scale caused by the new Grosvenor House, designed by Lutyens, consultant architect to the Grosvenor Estate.

ALDFORD HOUSE, built to the designs of Balfour and Turner for Sir Alfred Beit in 1897, was not widely admired by contemporaries. 'Beit House,' wrote an architectural journalist in 1909, 'remarkable for looking so much like what it is – the African lodge transplanted – is the most incongruous of all the incongruities of Park Lane. . . . How easily and how surely do these modern extravagances miss that distinction of sobriety, severity and reserve which is the key to the fascination of the old Town houses of the eighteenth century. . . .' It was one of the 'family houses' with which the Grosvenor Estate intended to replace the older houses in Park Lane, when planning redevelopment during Edward VII's reign. After 1919, the tenants for this type of house had disappeared or could find more than enough houses of this size elsewhere. Aldford House was demolished in 1931.

DORCHESTER HOUSE in 1928, the latest in date and the most self-conscious of the Park Lane mansions, and possibly the greatest loss. It was built in 1851–7, for the millionaire R. S. Holford, by Lewis Vulliamy (1791–1871), who had already carried out a number of commissions for Holford at Westonbirt. Holford was one of the richest and most influential of that group of Victorian *bourgeois* who were in a position to emulate the hereditary nobility as patrons of the arts.

'. . . this mansion', wrote the *Builder* in 1852, 'is built for long endurance. If the New Zealander who is to gaze on the deserted site of fallen London in some distant time to come, sees nothing else standing in the neighbourhood, he will certainly find the weather-tinted walls of Dorchester House . . .'

We can now see the cruel irony of Holford's care that his house should be constructed of the finest materials, but it is typical of the spirit in which he and Vulliamy approached the planning of the villa. It was modelled externally on the Villa Farnesina at Rome, built by Peruzzi about 1508; internally it was arranged to provide a magnificent background for a society which was not only rich but cultured, and well able to appreciate its design.

It was demolished in 1929, despite several abortive attempts to find a use for it, as an embassy, a museum or a centre for opera. A correspondent to *Country Life* observed: '. . . A country that lives on

capital, treating Death Duties as income, must not expect monuments of individualism to survive' – even 'a private palace of monumental construction and unusual beauty on one of the most pictorial sites in London.'

The Saloon in 1905 looked through the arcaded openings on to the great staircase, a solution traditionally suggested by Sir Edwin Landseer to Holford, who was unhappy at Vulliamy's idea of absorbing the western landing into the saloon. There were few more splendid settings for entertainment in London than this room, overlooking Park Lane and Hyde Park on one side, and connected to the rest of the magnificent reception rooms by the vaulted first-floor landing.

The great staircase hall in 1928, one of the main features of the house, seen from the first landing, carefully planned by Holford, as a *point de vue* for the ascending visitor. There was an open gallery round three sides, with vaulted and painted ceilings. The columns and frieze were carried out in that most contemporary of materials, Parian ware.

The Red Drawing-room in 1905, with the monumental marble fireplace designed by Alfred Stevens (1818–75). He did a number of other designs for decoration and furniture, showing himself to be as versatile as the Renaissance artists on whom he modelled his work.

The southern end of Park Lane in 1885: almost all the buildings shown here have disappeared in a series of demolitions which had repercussions not only on Park Lane itself, but also on the atmosphere of Hyde Park.

On the left, the row of modest terrace houses, which included an unusual 1847 Perpendicular Gothic house by Gilbert Scott's partner, W. M. Moffatt, were sold to Charles Clore in 1956 for just over half a million pounds and in due course were demolished for the building of the Hilton Hotel. This was unfortunate not so much because of the value of the houses which disappeared as because of the unsympathetic height and shape of the building which replaced them. The height of 311 feet and the enormously high plot ratio of 6:1, nearly twice the permitted plot ratio for the area, was sanctioned by the then Minister of Housing himself, on the grounds that an additional 700 hotel rooms for American and other tourists was essential to the national economy. This short-sighted decision has proved as disastrous to the Royal Parks as the Fine Art Commission predicted in 1957, when it warned of the prejudicial effect of such a building on Hyde Park, adding that it would then be virtually impossible to refuse permission for other exceptionally high buildings on the perimeter of the central Parks, and that the final result would be to destroy their unique pastoral character.

LONDONDERRY HOUSE. The first 'victim' of the Hilton decision was Londonderry House, the most important private house to disappear in London since the war, a particularly grand and aristocratic early nineteenth-century mansion. Even before the erection of the Hilton Hotel, it was not easy to find occupiers for such a house – with the Hilton Hotel to the north, and another lower tower to the south, Londonderry House was hopelessly over-shadowed, and its owners could argue that residential use in the proximity of two large hotels was impossible.

Though the house had – incredibly – been left off the original statutory lists of historic buildings, it was added in August 1959 to those lists. The London County Council considered making a Building Preservation Order, but this was never confirmed, partly because the Ministry's experts seem to have been lukewarm about Londonderry House, and even more because any local authority making a B.P.O. lays themselves open to a 'purchase notice', and a notice to purchase Londonderry House would have been embarras-sing – and expensive. In the sad event, Londonderry House was sold for redevelopment on 26 July 1962, for £500,000.

Originally Holdernesse House, it was designed by James 'Athenian' Stuart in 1760–5, for the d'Arcy family, and substantially remodelled in 1825–8 by Benjamin and Philip Wyatt, for the third Marquess of Londonderry. A good deal of Stuart's work survived the Wyatt remodelling, including the two rooms on the first floor overlooking the Park, though during the Second World War some of the Stuart decorations were whitewashed over, when the house was in use as as an L.C.C. depot.

Not only was it an important house architecturally, for over a century it was the scene of important political receptions. The Wyatts' staircase, '1825 at its grandest', comparable to any left in London, led into the ballroom, the finest room in the house, lined by the third Marquess's purchase of Canova statues, sold at Sotheby's in 1962.

HARCOURT HOUSE in 1838, showing the *porte cochère* and the high wall which so irritated its critics. It was built in the 1720s for Lord Bingley by Thomas Archer, one of the most uncompromisingly baroque of English architects. In 1736, a critic wrote of it as 'one of the most singular pieces of architecture about the town, . . . rather like a convent than the residence of a man of quality; in fact, it seems more like a copy of one of Poussin's landscape ornaments than a design to imitate any of the genuine beauties of buildings'. In 1825, Lord Harcourt lost a 99-year lease of the house at cards to the Duke of Portland, for whom Thomas Cundy did this elevation, and possibly added a fourth floor to Archer's house. The house stood behind a courtyard, in a manner common to the large houses which stood in squares, and behind the house itself was a large garden, concealed from view by more high walls, and groundglass and cast-iron screens, some 200 feet long by 80 feet high, erected by the fifth Duke, to shut out his neighbours' gaze, as he had done at his country house at Welbeck Abbey.

The house's gloomy fascination was increased by its occupation by the eccentric fifth Duke of Portland. These drawings, showing the entrance hall and his own sitting room, were done after his death, in 1880. Unfashionable in style, large and with spacious grounds, the house remained empty and was an obvious victim for redevelopment. It was demolished in 1906.

CHESTERFIELD HOUSE, built for the famous Earl of Chesterfield in 1749–52, by Isaac Ware. It faced down Great Stanhope
Street to Stanhope Gate, and even after the garden had been truncated for the building of Chesterfield Gardens in 1870, it remained
one of the finest houses in London. Its last occupants were the
Princess Royal and the Earl of Harewood, so it can hardly be said
to have been unfashionable. It was demolished in 1937.

The columns and the grand staircase came from the Duke of
Chandos' house at Canons Park, demolished in 1744 to pay some
of the family's debts.

'My court, my Hall and my staircase will really be magnificent,'
wrote the Earl to a friend. 'The staircase particularly will form such
a scene, as is not in England. The expense will ruin me, but the
enjoyment will please me.' On the house's demolition, the staircase
was used for a cinema in Broadstairs, where it was bombed during
the War.

Robert Adam was a remarkably prolific and fashionable architect, who built not only the Adelphi and several other speculative streets, but also altered and remodelled more than a dozen important London houses for the aristocracy and gentry – of these not more than three remain standing unaltered. LANSDOWNE HOUSE, on the south side of Berkeley Square, begun for Lord Bute and finished for Lord Shelburne in 1762–8, was one of the most important. It was reduced to a travesty of its former self in 1936 when the front was set back some 20 feet and rebuilt. Some of the interior was preserved, though other important rooms were sold to museums abroad. Its mutilation followed on the destruction of the east side, where Lord Bearsted had purchased Nos 12–19, in the Square, and the adjoining six houses in Bruton Street, including No. 17, an extremely fine eighteenth-century town mansion, in the early 1930s for redevelopment. Their demolition was followed by that of the houses further south in 1937 for the building of the Air Ministry. Other houses, including No. 38, belonging to Lord Rosebery, have gone elsewhere, and the only eighteenth-century houses left, Nos 42–52, were saved by a Preservation Order in 1963, followed by a hard-fought Public Inquiry.

HAREWOOD HOUSE was remodelled by Adam for the Duke of Roxburghe in 1776. It stood on the north-east corner of Hanover Square, fronting on to the square and to Holles Place. The 'Eating-Room' on the ground floor was particularly fine. Its last aristocratic occupant was the Earl of Harewood, who sold it to the Royal Agricultural Society for offices in 1895. None the less, the internal details and the fine plasterwork were largely untouched when the house was demolished in 1915.

No. 180 QUEEN'S GATE was one of four houses built by Norman Shaw between 1875 and 1888 on the east side of the street. No. 180 was demolished by the Imperial College as part of its plans for expansion published in 1955. The Victorian Society appealed to the architects, Norman and Dawbarn, in 1958, only to be told that it was already too late to modify the scheme. The impotence of public planning authorities in the face of a determined institution is shown by the fruitless battle to save this house which went on for over ten years. The planning authorities were unwilling to serve a Building Preservation Order to force the College to keep the house, while the latter and their architects, who can hardly have been unaware of the rising tide of public concern, were not apparently prepared to consider any alternative scheme. When, in 1969, the College applied for formal permission to demolish No. 180, they claimed that they had no alternative site left for their computer centre. This case shows the extreme danger of long-term planning schemes without flexibility or room for imaginative preservation, where it is impossible to re-assess proposed demolitions in the light of changes in public taste, or even planning law. Thus the Victorian Society pointed out in vain in 1969 that 'there was now a greater awareness of the value of the best Victorian buildings and also an increasing need to conserve what remains of the distinctive fabric of Victorian and earlier London in view of the speed of redevelopment and the loss of so many notable buildings elsewhere'.

The drawing-room in 1956, when the house was still in the occupation of the Makins family for whom it was built in 1883. Many of the interiors were unaltered with their original Morris wallpapers, and most of their original fireplaces. When the house was finally demolished in 1970, no apparent effort was made by the College to salvage the interiors, and arrangements had to be made with the demolition contractors, with the inevitable loss of many fine things.

The City in 1710, showing Wren's churches soon after they were
built.

'. . . this united group of church towers, each of which ministers to
the other by counterpoint of form, by playing change of outline,
and variety of form, Wren was so careful in planning, that no two
similar outlines neighbour each other; seldom has he placed together two steeples in equal strength of tone . . .' Without breaking
the bounds of architectural propriety, or disgracing dignity of form,
Wren has given us, in his fifty-three churches, as many varieties of
steeple outline; . . . The result of calm choice of individual form,
combined with severe discipline in imaginative composition, shows
itself in each one of these masterpieces of architectural design.'
A. H. Mackmurdo: 1883.

# II
# CHURCHES

Wren's City Churches

London's great loss in the last hundred years has been amongst her Wren churches in the City itself. The peculiar tragedy of this destruction was that the whole was so much greater than the sum of the parts. In the words of A. H. Mackmurdo, writing in 1883 : '. . . . this characteristic of unity in design is then the first and most important of these City Churches, a characteristic which gives to London an interest above that enjoyed by any Continental town . . . from the tower of St Saviour's, Southwark, the entire group is to be seen, and I know of no more magnificent sight . . . this view of London, wrapt in her day-dark halo of earth cloud . . . the pale cathedral lifting itself aloft – a miracle of unmoved dignity, boldly central among her square massive mansions, and huge blocks of seven-storied offices; its dome as soft in outline, as tender in graduated light, as any summer cloud, yet standing not alone, but surrounded by her daughter churches, whose steeples blazon the sky with pinnacles of sable and silver – a most lovely sight'.

Mackmurdo added that, once having seen this panorama, 'We look upon all these churches as so intimately connected one with another, that St Paul's, bereft of its surrounding steeples, is to us as a parent bereft of her children – a Niobe in architecture.'

The problem of the City churches first raised its head over a century ago, in the 1850s, when the City's population began to fall dramatically in proportion to that of Greater London. Wren had rebuilt fifty-three of the eighty-seven churches destroyed in the Fire, of which only four had disappeared by 1850, and with forty-nine almost empty churches on valuable sites in the City, it was thought by the ecclesiastical authorities to be more difficult to raise funds for building and staffing churches in the godless suburbs.

In 1854, the Bishop of London therefore drew up a list of twenty-nine churches which he proposed to demolish. This list was a little haphazard, and seems to have been ill considered as it included not only a number of Wren's finest works, admittedly unfashionable in ecclesiological circles where Gothic was all the rage, but also St Helen Bishopsgate and All Hallows Staining, both dating from before the Great Fire. It would be impossible to give a complete list of those threatened, but it included St Mildred Bread Street, St Swithin, and St Mary Abchurch, all with domed interiors, the rare Gothic St Mary Aldermary and St Alban Wood Street, as well as churches chiefly remarkable for their carved interiors such as St Peter Cornhill and All Hallows Lombard Street.

A rising tide of public protest against this proposal, which even *The Times*, in principle a supporter of the measure, could not but call a 'vast act of desecration', saved a large number of the churches. Fortunately, not everyone could contemplate with equanimity the prospect that: '. . . church, steeple, bells, organ, minister, clerk, beadle, sexton, pulpit, pews, will all give way to nothing worse, we will hope, than dry goods, woollens, prints, tallow candles, stationery, and such profane material. The neat little architectural façade, the three or four modest windows of the basest Gothic or the tamest Italian; the church-door beset with parish and tax-gatherers' notices, and the brief interruption to the otherwise continuous line of shopfronts, will all be missed . . .'

Despite the considerable public protest, the Union of Benefices Act was obtained in 1860, under which a total of fourteen churches were destroyed by 1888, and a further eight since. Although the ranks of Tuscany, in the form of those committed mediaevalists, G. E. Street and William Morris, did in fact protest over the removal of Wren's churches, their adherents committed almost as great a desecration by 'improving' the interiors of those churches which escaped destruction. This petty remodelling involved the removal of the great carved box pews, particularly at the east end to make room for a choir, and the substitution of draughty open pews, often in unsuitable pitch pine, the resiting of the pulpits, many originally of the three-decker variety, and in the removal of the ornamental swags and carving.

In 1926 a further attempt to reduce the number of City churches was made, based on the Phillimore Report of 1919, under which nineteen churches were to be demolished. These included Wren's St Magnus, St Mary-at-Hill, St Vedast Foster Lane, and eight others, St Mary Woolnoth, Hawksmoor's only City church, and three churches by the Dances, father and son, including St Botolph Aldersgate Street. A measure to facilitate the removal of churches, by obviating the need for consent by the inhabitants of the parish, was put before Parliament, but was fortunately defeated by the protests of a large number of private citizens, as well as by the official opposition of the City Corporation itself.

This represented a great triumph for those in favour of the preservation of London's architectural heritage, a group fortunately gaining in numbers and influence in the period between the wars. Only one church was in fact removed instead of the nineteen proposed.

However, this, one of the greatest victories for the forces of conservation, was rendered fruitless by the Second World War. Some fourteen years later, the Blitz damaged or destroyed twenty of the forty-seven churches of all periods remaining in the City. Predictably, it was decided not to rebuild eight, many of which were on the list of those it was planned to remove in 1926. These included St Anne and St Agnes, St Alban Wood Street, St Stephen Coleman Street, St Dunstan-in-the-East and St Nicholas Cole Abbey. Even where magnificent efforts at reconstruction have been carried out, the total loss of the original interiors has left little more than a series of pastiches. St Andrew-by-the-Wardrobe, St Lawrence Jewry and St Mary-le-Bow, totally burnt out in 1940, are really only 'Wren' churches in name, as far as the interiors are concerned.

Outside the City, history has been repeating itself, as the redundant churches are now to be found in the nineteenth-century inner suburbs, so anxiously provided with churches by Victorian bishops and benefactors. In consequence, a number of Blitz casualties in these areas have not been repaired, and other churches have been secularised, rather than being demolished.

It would not be possible to include more than a representative handful of those churches abandoned or demolished since 1945, and this is a continuing process, leading not only to the demolition of churches on suburban sites, now as valuable as those in the City once were, but also to the reorganisation and 'modernisation' of their interiors. No one would wish either the Church of England or any other ecclesiastical body to be prevented from carrying out its primary functions because of the need to preserve outdated buildings, but the way in which some important and interesting churches have been treated has given rise to justifiable concern.

In general, the Established Church has improved its mechanism for protecting churches from demolition, decay and neglect, or the destruction of their interiors by well-meaning 'restoration'. None the less, it still maintains its exemption from governmental control, first obtained in 1913, when the Ancient Monuments Act was passed, under the more recent and effective legislation for the protection of important and historic buildings. Today perhaps it is the numerous Victorian churches which are at risk, rather than the depleted numbers of seventeenth- and eighteenth-century 'God-boxes' so despised by the Victorians themselves. It is perhaps not yet generally accepted in diocesan circles that the whitewashing of a carefully planned Victorian polychromatic interior is as serious a crime as the tearing out of box-pews and the turned balusters of a Georgian altar-rail.

This exemption from planning laws extends to both Roman Catholic and Nonconformist churches, neither of which has the rudimentary machinery of the Church of England for the protection of buildings which, though privately owned, have public importance as works of art. Despite the goodwill and interest evinced by many ecclesiastical authorities, the situation is still so unsatisfactory that it is not surprising that there is a growing feeling amongst those concerned with the protection of ancient buildings that statutory protection may be necessary. It is after all fairly generally accepted that the public have an interest in and a right to protect important historic buildings in private ownership : it is a little absurd to exempt from protection that class of buildings upon which more pious generations than our own expended such a large proportion of their wealth and artistic talent.

ST MARY MAGDALENE OLD FISH STREET, during demolition in 1886, showing its very unusual steeple with a lantern topped by a vase, on five octagonal steps.

ST DIONIS BACKCHURCH,
demolished in 1878. It stood on
the west side of Lime Street, just
north of Fenchurch Street. This
picture shows how very much
more striking the churches were
amid the lower buildings of the
Victorian city.

The interior showing the ornate, yet elegant pulpit, and the original
woodwork and the monuments of which it has a remarkable collection. Together with the font cover (not shown here) made in the
shape of a tower, the woodwork was used for the new church of St
Dionis at Parsons Green.

ALL HALLOWS THE GREAT AND LESS about 1890. Its curious name records the amalgamation of two pre-Fire parishes in 1666. It had one of the only two screens in the post-Fire churches, in this case the gift of Theodore Jacobsen, a merchant from the Steelyard whose Hanseatic eagle appears on both screen and pulpit. Happily the screen was moved to St Margaret Lothbury when it was demolished in 1894. The tower and the north aisle had been pulled down ten years earlier to widen Upper Thames Street.

ST MILDRED POULTRY. Standing next to the Poultry Compter, one of the debtors' prisons, it was the last resting place for a number of inmates. It was one of the first churches to go under the Act of 1860, being demolished in 1872. A Lincolnshire gentleman passing down the Poultry was shocked to see it being demolished, and bought the stones for re-erection at his estate near Louth.

The agricultural recession intervened, and the church, transported by barge to Louth, was never rebuilt. Some of the stones have been used for garden walls, most remain in a pile in the orchard.

ST MATTHEW FRIDAY STREET was demolished in 1884, and Mackmurdo describes how he found it:
'Posted all over with placards inviting tenders for the purchase of its materials. . . . Instead of a deserted church, we shall find, on visiting its site, a superbly ornamented warehouse, standing staunch and strong on its cast iron legs, proud of its "practical" offices and shoplike display of cheap art, deign it to have any show of art at all. The exigencies of trade . . . !'

CHRIST CHURCH NEWGATE about 1890, showing the original pews, and the two pulpits, one obtained from the Temple Church in 1840. That on the right, the original, was unique in having religious subjects carved on the panels. This was later broken up, when the church was repewed, and incorporated in the choir stalls. Firemen busy in the ruins of Christ Church after the great fire-bomb raid of Christmas week, 1940, in which the interiors of St Lawrence Jewry and St Bride, Fleet Street, also perished. Christ Church, which acted as chapel for Christ's Hospital, is not to be rebuilt.

ST NICHOLAS COLE ABBEY, on the list for demolition in both 1854 and 1919, and finally burnt out in 1941. This photograph, taken about 1890, shows some of the alterations to the furnishings and decorations. Later on the pulpit was removed and the swags over the windows were removed and texts stencilled on to the walls. The church is still standing but the interior is, of course, new.

The west end of ST MILDRED BREAD STREET, the only unaltered Wren interior to survive the improvers, destroyed in 1941 and not rebuilt. It had a dome and some of the finest plasterwork of any of the City churches.

DUTCH CHURCH, AUSTIN FRIARS. One of the City's few mediaeval churches, the remains of the great conventual church of the Grey Friars, with a characteristic wide 'preaching nave', from a print of about 1825. The church was built about 1350, and given after the Dissolution to Protestant refugees from the Low Countries. The choir and steeple were demolished in 1611, but the rest escaped the Great Fire. In 1862 the roof was burnt and replaced, and in 1940 it was destroyed by a direct hit. Of the other mediaeval City churches, All Hallows Barking was burnt in 1941.

**ST MARY
ALDERMANBURY** in 1928.
An extremely plain church, whose
interior had been thoroughly re-
organised. Woodthorpe's Venetian
tracery of 1864 can be seen in the
side windows.

It was burnt out in 1940, leaving
only the east end with its 'grossly
oversized, very jolly and proud
scrolls' and its pillars standing.

The ruins were shipped to Fulton,
Missouri, where they have been
re-erected. The Blitz did not
affect only the City churches, and
again for some churches it was
the occasion rather than the real
cause of their disappearance.

ST PETER REGENT SQUARE in 1950, showing the portico which survived the bombing in the Second World War. It was a "Commissioners' Church" built in 1822–6 by William and H. W. Inwood, the same father and son partnership which was responsible for St Pancras New Church in Euston Square. Despite representations by the Georgian Group, who wanted the portico retained even if the church was abandoned, the portico was finally demolished in 1954 and the site sold.

History repeated itself on the other side of the square, where William Tite had built a church in 1824–7 for a Presbyterian congregation, then under the pastorship of Edward Irving, later to become famous as the founder of the Catholic Apostolic Church. Here the Bath stone towers, a miniature version of York Minster, survived the war damage of February 1945, but again, despite the urging of the Victorian Society, the church authorities preferred to demolish all that remained.

ST JOHN RED LION SQUARE, one of J. L. Pearson's best churches, built 1874. It suffered badly in the bombing, and worse, according to one account, afterwards. In the vicar's words: 'Rolls and rolls of lead from the roof were sent to a dump; beautiful wrought-iron grilles were torn from perfectly sound arches, ready for the scrap heap; and if constant appeals had not been made to the diocesan surveyor, all would have gone.' All finally went after some years, and the church was entirely demolished.

ST ANSELM AND ST CECILIA SARDINIA STREET was first established as a Roman Catholic chapel in 1687 during the reign of James II, when the penal laws against Catholics went unenforced. On the flight of James II, the chapel was sacked by an anti-Catholic mob, but was re-established as a place of worship under the protection of first the Portuguese Embassy at 54 Lincoln's Inn Fields, and after 1723 of the Sardinian Embassy, which gave its name to both the chapel and the street in which it stood. After an accidental fire, in 1759 it was rebuilt in the Italian manner to the designs of Signor Jean-Baptist Jacque, the ambassador's secretary.

The interior of the Sardinian Chapel in 1808. The ambassador had a pew in the north-east end of the chancel gallery.

In the course of the nineteenth century the chapel became the Church of St Anselm and St Cecilia, independent of any foreign embassy. The interior was pewed, and the rails which separated the large chancel from the nave were moved up to form a square enclosure for the high altar.

The west end of the church about 1907. It was destroyed for the Kingsway scheme of 1909.

THE SURREY CHAPEL in Blackfriars Road about 1890, an unusual eighteenth-century octagonal place of worship, built by the Rev. Rowland Hill in 1782. It was finally closed as a chapel in 1881, and then became a factory, and later a boxing arena, known as 'The Ring'. It was badly damaged in the Second World War and demolished.

The interior, about 1812.

THE CITY TEMPLE in Holborn Viaduct, 1874, built to the design of Lockwood and Mawson in what was termed the 'light Italian style'. It remained one of the most important of London Nonconformist churches until the Second World War, when it was bombed. It was built to replace the Poultry Chapel, built in 1819 on part of the site of the Poultry Compter, which had one of the oldest Nonconformist congregations in the City. This congregation was begun in 1640 in Anchor Lane, Lower Thames Street, and moved a number of times before 1819. In 1869 Dr Joseph Parker became minister and became so successful, and his congregation so large, that it was necessary to move. The Poultry Chapel was bought by the London Joint Bank, and demolished for the new headquarters of the Midland Bank.

# III
# QUARTIERS

Strand and Fleet Street

The Strand is one of the oldest streets in London, with buildings from all periods of its history, including a much mutilated Roman Bath.

The destruction of the eastern end began in 1878 with the removal of Temple Bar as a traffic obstruction. It was erected in 1672, reputedly to the design of Sir Christopher Wren. Here it is in 1875 looking east towards Fleet Street and the City. The hoarding on the left is round the site of the Royal Courts of Justice, erected 1874–82 to the designs of G. E. Street.

The western end of the Strand has been extensively developed since 1930, with the loss of several irreplaceable buildings. The major remaining block at the Trafalgar Square end is under threat as this books goes to press.

The making of Kingsway was the most important 'metropolitan improvement' of the last hundred years, comparable to that of Regent Street. It was undeniably necessary, and is still, indeed, one of the few barely adequate north–south routes in London, yet it was responsible for the devastation of a larger area than any other previous event but the Great Fire. This devastation was not confined, in the words of the *Architectural Review*, to the loss of 'an intensely interesting, if somewhat squalid, sector of Old London', but also contributed to the later destruction of Bloomsbury, and probably to that of Rennie's Waterloo Bridge. It also proved difficult to let the important new sites on the new thoroughfare, many of which remained vacant for over ten years after King Edward and Queen Alexandra opened the new street in 1905.

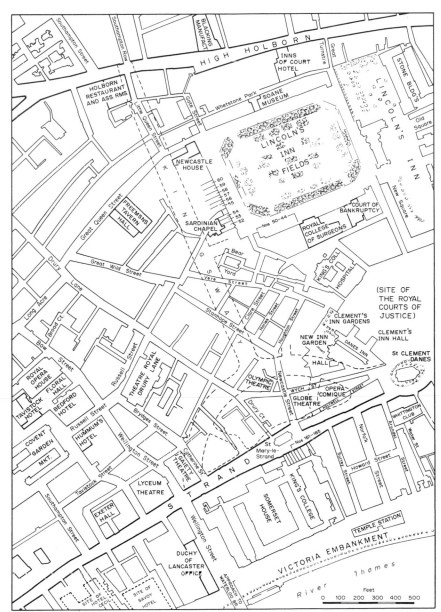

*Sketch map of the Strand c. 1870. The superimposed lines indicate the present line of Aldwych and Kingsway. Buildings discussed in the text appear in bold caps.*

St Mary-le-Strand, about 1890. On the left was the entrance to Holywell Street, famous for Booksellers' Row. All the houses on the left were swept away, to form a new island site. Contemporary opinion praised the decision to route the new street to preserve both St Mary's and St Clement Danes seen on the far right.

Further east along the Strand, between St Mary's and St Clement Danes, showing houses on the north side of the Strand, also demolished.

Old houses on the south side of Wych Street, about 1890. The Globe and Opera Comique theatres occupied much of the rest of the south side; Danes Inn and New Inn, the north. Holywell and Wych Streets were demolished about 1900. Their removal meant the loss of many early Georgian tiled and plastered houses. A number of other buildings were removed in the interests of road-widening or redevelopment.

Nos 164–7 The Strand in 1886. These four seventeenth-century houses were not only timber-fronted, something forbidden in London under the Acts passed after the Fire, but also largely timber-framed. With their carved fronts and elaborate fenestration, they provided the largest and most picturesque group in the Strand until 1893, when the two left-hand houses were demolished. The others survived until 1966, when they were pulled down to make way for an extension to King's College. Nos 414 and 415, further west, were also of the Restoration period, and survived until 1911.

The Duchy of Lancaster Office and Lancaster Place in 1900, showing the dignified early nineteenth-century approach to the Strand from Rennie's Waterloo Bridge. The Office and terrace were designed by Sir Robert Smirke, surveyor to the Duchy in 1823. The ironwork with the rose motif was particularly successful. The terrace and Office were rebuilt in 1928–30.

Detail of ironwork.

# Lincoln's Inn Fields

Lincoln's Inn Fields was laid out between 1640 and 1657, and is therefore one of the earliest 'squares' in London, with an important and varied series of large individual houses on its three sides, which have been sadly depleted in the last fifty years.

Nos 54 and 55 in 1900, part of a group which ran from No. 2 Portsmouth Street to No. 56 Lincoln's Inn Fields, showing the arched entrance to old Sardinia Street. Originally this whole row, and also Nos 57–60, were to have been demolished and rebuilt fronting on to the new Kingsway. Remonstrations were made, however, to the L.C.C., including one from the Society for the Protection of Ancient Buildings, signed by Alma Tadema, Waterhouse, Webb, Sargent and Walter Besant amongst others, and the last four houses were reprieved. Nos 54 and 53, dating from the mid-seventeenth century, were the Portuguese Embassy, to which the 'Sardinian Chapel' (pages 68–9) was originally attached. These houses were demolished in 1912.

A number of other important buildings have been lost since. Nos 66 and 67, Newcastle House, was largely reconstructed by Lutyens in 1930, depriving it of much of its historical interest. On the north side, the Lincoln's Inn Heraldic Office, a Georgian building suitably Gothicised, where heraldic research and painting had been carried on for 200 years, was compulsorily purchased by the L.C.C. in 1951 and demolished for road widening.

Recently, the worst losses have been on the south side. No. 35 (below), originally a pair with No. 36, was designed by Sir Robert Taylor in 1754. It had a very interesting fenestration with a hexagonal theme which was repeated in the door panels and the internal woodwork. It was destroyed by enemy action.

No. 35 had several fine rooms and a very large staircase compartment with a fine elliptical stair with elaborate ironwork.

Nos 44–50 in 1911.

This was inevitable, but the destruction of Nos 44–50, a large and important group of early eighteenth-century houses, after the Second World War, was quite deliberate. They were first threatened in 1947, when they were listed Grade II, being then described as 'houses of interesting design dating from the early eighteenth century. There have been some alterations, but they remain a picturesque survival of the early appearance of the square and their loss . . . would be most regrettable.' Internally, they were even more important, containing contemporary decorative features such as staircases, panelling, fireplaces and painted ceilings.

The finest of the group were Nos 44 and 46, recognised as important in 1911, when, though preservation was less feasible legally, there were in fact many more early Georgian houses extant in London for comparison.

The Royal College of Surgeons occupied a fine block by Barry, somewhat mutilated, at Nos 39–43, and after the war they applied for outline permission to extend to east and west. Planning permission was given in June 1948 provided satisfactory detailed plans were submitted within six months. This was done for the site to the east, Nos 35–8, but not for the remaining houses which, together with the Old Curiosity Shop, extended to Portugal Street. Meanwhile, the College pursued a policy of buying up these houses and converting them, the interior of No. 44 being gravely damaged in the process, and robbed of much of its historical interest. In 1957, the College formally gave notice of its intention to demolish Nos 44, 45 and 46, the last of which they proposed to purchase from a well-known firm of solicitors. The proposal was that the College, and the Imperial Cancer Research Fund already connected with it, should build more accommodation, and that in due course the recently founded College of General Practitioners should demolish the other three houses. Pressure was put on the Government to agree quickly, since the College claimed that it was not easy for the solicitors to find alternative accommodation, that the interiors had been so mutilated – by the College – as to be of little further interest, and that money given for cancer research had been spent on the purchase of the sites. The L.C.C. felt that the houses, though damaged, were still extremely valuable as examples of early Georgian interiors, and also had a good deal to contribute as a terrace of mixed housing. However, the argument that it was essential to build more cancer research laboratories on those very sites was never seriously challenged and Nos 44–6 were demolished in 1959. With those three houses gone, the arguments for saving Nos 48–50 vanished and they too were torn down in 1967.

No. 46. The staircase and hall, 1957.

No. 45. Room on the ground floor in 1906.

## The London Square

London's particular contribution to urban planning is the *quartier des carrés*, a name originally applied to Bloomsbury, but equally applicable to Belgravia, St Marylebone or even Mayfair.

'The English square or crescent . . . is a restricted whole as complete as the courtyard of a convent. They form fine geometrical figures in the town plan, they are regular and completely uniform on all sides, and a series of such squares may be linked together in any order . . . It is as if the traditions of the Middle Ages had been handed down to the present day in the squares, these domestic quarters. But the narrow courts of the old town have been transformed into the open squares of the newer quarters. . . .' (S. E. Rassmussen: *London: The Unique City*).

Even as Rassmussen wrote in the early 1930s the destruction of these same squares had begun, and has gathered momentum in the intervening forty years, so that today of the thirty or so squares in Central London and the West End, only three are undamaged, with the unity of their façades unbroken. Any classical architectural form is, of course, peculiarly vulnerable to minor alteration, but the destruction of important London squares has gone far beyond this. However, the argument that even minor alteration can cause irreparable damage has been stood on its head by developers and other interested parties who urge that once the unity of the square has been spoiled the rest might as well be demolished. Even since the institution of listing and planning control in 1947, this point has been made with success in half a dozen instances where major groups were concerned.

## Bloomsbury

Bloomsbury was one of the most carefully planned of the great London estates. Built between 1776 and 1860, the Bedford Estate Office provided the ground plans and in some cases the elevations of the houses, but throughout co-ordinated and controlled the work of many different developers and builders. Traffic also was controlled, through traffic and heavy commercial traffic having no business in the estate being excluded by strategically placed gates. This concept of a residential precinct in which people can live agreeably has recently been discovered by modern town planners, but protective gates were common in nineteenth-century London from Highbury to Pimlico. Over fifty-five were removed by the London County Council in 1890 and 1893, in the name of progress. The removal of its gates was the *coup-de-grâce* for residential Bloomsbury. The eastern side of the Bedford Estate, Southampton Row, Russell Square and Tavistock Square, has been turned over to hotels and office blocks, while the western edge has been destroyed by two great cultural institutions, the British Museum and London University.

Since 1945, the pace of change in the London University precinct has accelerated, resulting in the total destruction of one of the most important neighbourhood plans in London, and the demolition of a number of buildings which would not, I suspect, have been allowed to fall to less intellectually respectable bulldozers. The whole problem of Bloomsbury came to a head over the demolition of the second phase of Woburn Square in 1969, and is a very good example of the total pointlessness and impotence of most public outcry in the face of a large and determined institution. It is also a good example of the way in which it is usually possible for such an institution, and London University is not unique in using such claims, to argue that, firstly, valuable public money has been invested in the site, on the assumption that development would be allowed, and, secondly, that some outline plan, in this case over thirty years old, sanctioned the development in question.

London University was faced in 1969 with a revolt among some of its senior members, and published an advertisement on 18 February putting forward its own case, which claimed, *inter alia*, that some of the property was acquired in 1927, and that planning permission for the erection of new buildings on the west side of Woburn Square was given as long ago as 1932 (a period at which Georgian architecture was held in such high regard that there was a proposal afoot to demolish the whole west side of Bedford Square to relieve traffic congestion). More tenably, it claimed that the Martin plan for the development of the University precinct, published in 1957, would have been irreparably damaged by any attempt to preserve Woburn Square.

However, even in 1957, when the Martin Plan was published, the L.C.C., the planning authority, could do little to object since it was long established that the University had 'over-riding claims'. In any case outline permission had been granted in 1938, long before any historic buildings legislation, for the rebuilding of the block north of Montague Place.

It is therefore London University and its architects that must bear the responsibility for deciding to destroy Gordon Square and its ancillary streets, Gordon and Taviton Streets, parts of Gower Street, the west side of Russell Square and, finally, both Torrington and

Woburn Squares, either of which could have provided an almost collegiate heart to the precinct, had this been what the University and its architects wanted. A considerable number of the buildings were listed by the Ministry of Housing in 1947, and Sir Leslie Martin recommended the retention of some of the older buildings in his report. Only two groups are in fact guaranteed preservation, both on the edge of the precinct, the west side of Tavistock Square and a group on the corner of Bedford Square, one of the three undamaged London squares.

Bloomsbury in 1963, showing how the pattern of linked squares is being eroded. On the bottom right next to the British Museum can be seen one of the few original blocks remaining, between Montague Street and Bedford Place. To the north is Russell Square, whose east side has been totally rebuilt. The scale of the new University buildings is given by the large white stone Senate House on the left and the brick blocks to the north. Since this photograph was taken, almost all the Regency terrace houses immediately north of Russell Square have been demolished, from the west side of Woburn Square to the east side of Bedford Place. They are to be replaced by blocks which will so disrupt the original scheme as to wreck the finest and most extensive example of aristocratic estate planning in London.

Endsleigh Street Gate in 1893, looking north to Euston Square. The whole of the right side of the street, built during the 1830s by Thomas Cubitt, has gone since the Second World War. The gardens to the south side of Euston Square, originally similar to those of Eaton Square, were divorced from the houses they served by an enterprising developer in 1920, and built over. This was one of the acts of vandalism which provoked the London Squares Act of 1923.

The five top-hatted gate-keepers on retirement in 1893.

The east side of Tavistock Square in 1911, built by James Burton in 1800. The last part of Burton's terrace was demolished in 1938, at the same time as the north side.

Woburn Square in 1969. The square was built by the Sim family about 1829, after they had completed the parallel and similar Torrington Square. Christ Church, built at the same time to the design of Lewis Vulliamy, is also threatened. Four houses in the Square were destroyed in the war, the other thirty-five were listed buildings. The group shown here on the west side were demolished in 1970. Only a small group at the north end of the east side are now left.

Russell Square was held in 1826 to be 'one of the largest and most handsome in London'. Much of the east side was demolished between 1894 and 1911 for the erection of the Imperial and other hotels. The façades of the north and south sides were 'modernised' at the same period. Perhaps the most distinguished side was the west, shown here, built about 1810, now being gradually demolished by London University.

## Regent Street

London is of course a city designed and laid out by speculators, rather than by royal command or on lines approved by the Government. There was one great exception to this – Nash's great complex extending from the royal palace of Carlton House to the royal park of St Marylebone; even here, however, the building of Regent Street was managed much more like a private speculation than a government development plan. Its destruction came about for the same reason, because the Crown Estate Commissioners who managed the estate thought, like the agents and trustees of any other large estate, in terms of redevelopment once a century. As the original eighty-year leases expired, therefore, Nash's buildings were torn down and rebuilt, a fate only narrowly escaped by his Regent's Park terraces and Carlton House Terrace.

Nash himself lived at No. 14, on the right next to Carlton Street, a magnificent and skilfully planned building which contained not only Nash's own apartments but his office and a gallery some 70 feet long for the display of his copies of Raphael's pictures and famous Hellenistic sculptures. These two houses were demolished between 1921 and 1927.

St Philip's Chapel on the west side of Lower Regent Street, designed like much of this block by G. S. Repton, the younger son of Humphrey Repton, who worked in Nash's office for many years. The façade of the church was integrated with that of the street. It was demolished for the building of Carlton House in 1904.

Piccadilly Circus from the east in 1909, after the removal of the original north-east block (which stood on the site of the public lavatories) when Shaftesbury Avenue was created. This destroyed the small intimate southern Regent Circus, and created an unwieldy and inelegant open space which still presents a major headache for London's town planners.

The east side of Regent Street north of Beak Street in 1910. Robinson and Cleaver's new building of 1903 shows the new scale to which the street was to be rebuilt.

Looking north from Piccadilly Circus, 1910. The County Fire Office
was rebuilt with the rest of the Circus in the 1920s.

Regent Street, east side, looking
south.

# Abingdon Street

Abingdon Street, Westminster, was demolished together with part of No. 5 Old Palace Yard, by the Ministry of Works between 1943 and 1964. It provides a cautionary tale for anyone hoping to challenge any official scheme.

It continued the destruction of the older parts of Westminster round the Houses of Parliament, for Government offices, for roads or official open spaces, all desirable objectives which have been pursued so vigorously that Spring Gardens, Carrington House, Montagu House, Whitehall Place, Whitehall Gardens, Millbank Street, parts of Smith Square and its neighbourhood have all disappeared. Now we are told that Richmond Terrace, the rump of Parliament Street, and even the Foreign and Local Government Offices, and New Scotland Yard are all in jeopardy.

Abingdon Street was a mixed terrace of Georgian houses of which the central block was by Isaac Ware (*seen above opposite*), facing on to Victoria Tower Gardens. In 1938, the George V Memorial Committee proposed that Nos 5, 6 and 7 Old Palace Yard, (by Vardy) and Nos 28–9 Abingdon Street should be razed to provide a site for the statue of George V, and to expose the fourteenth-century Jewel House to public view. The Government offered to give the sites, while the other corporate owners in the street, the Ecclesiastical Commissioners and the civil servants' union, were ready to take this opportunity to redevelop their property. The newly formed Georgian Group took No. 27 as a 'Protest Office' with such success that after only two days of public signature of their petition the Memorial Committee withdrew its proposal.

However, the terrace suffered bomb damage, and subsequent decay from wind and weather, and the convenient decision was taken not to reinstate it, though Nos 24–7 were listed after the war by the Ministry of Housing's historic experts. In 1954 the Ministry of Works announced its intention to demolish No. 5 Old Palace Yard, which formed part of a group with Nos 6 and 7, for many years the residence of the Victorian politician, Henry Labouchere (1798–1869). The excuse for this was that 'a pledge had been given in 1939 by the Prime Minister to the Memorial Committee that the house would be pulled down' and a similar undertaking had been given to the Dean when a new Canon's house had been built behind it.

This is a curious story of official vandalism, the result of which is a rather unsatisfactory open space over a car park, and a rather gloomy and paper-filled pool in front of the Jewel House, a poor exchange for a row of houses as historic and interesting as any left in Westminster after the destruction of Whitehall Gardens between the wars. It also shows the attention paid by government officials to public protest.

## Carlton Mews

Carlton Mews, designed by Nash to serve the aristocratic inhabitants of Carlton House Terrace, was a most distinguished and unusual mews on three storeys: carriages on the ground floors, horses on the first floor reached by a paved ramp, and, above, one or two floors of living accommodation.

Like other mews, Carlton Mews was converted into houses, but otherwise, in 1945 after the Second World War, it was virtually intact, though threatened like the rest of the area by a Government proposal to demolish Carlton House Terrace itself.

In addition to its own attractive qualities, the Mews had the charm of surprise – the passer-by could turn off Cockspur Street, through a narrow entry, and there was the double-height mews complete with its tree'd court.

It was originally listed Grade III, but recommended for the Statutory List in 1968. Unfortunately, however, the Mews was the property of the Crown Estate Commissioners, no longer under the direct control of the Crown, but a partial subsidiary of the Ministry of Works, who like other government departments are not subject to planning legislation. Though they do consult the local authority as a matter of courtesy this is frequently done so discreetly that public opinion has no opportunity to make itself felt until too late.

Thus with Carlton Mews: in 1950 the United Services Club applied for outline permission to demolish five stables to build a ladies' annexe, for which they had obtained a building lease some two years before. This was granted by the London County Council, but nothing further occurred until early in 1959, when the Club revived the scheme and applied for full planning permission, then considerable public outcry ensued. Despite remonstrances from the Fine Art Commission and the L.C.C., not to say angry tenants in the Mews, the Crown Estate Commissioners expressed pained surprise that any such body should consider the Mews so important that it would be necessary to forgo the profitable economic development of the surrounding area. In any case the United Services Club were acting quite legitimately on the planning permission granted in 1951, and would have had to be compensated for the withdrawal of permission.

At this stage, someone at the L.C.C. seems to have decided to throw the baby out with the bath water and approve the U.S.C. plan for the demolition of five stables provided that the Crown Estates produced a comprehensive redevelopment scheme for knocking down the whole Mews. This was far from unacceptable to the Commissioners, ready to go into partnership with a private developer, and prepared to agree that the best way of meeting the anticipated public criticism of partial demolition was to promote a scheme for comprehensive redevelopment.

A further motive for the rebuilding of the Carlton Mews, admittedly of low density and a nonconforming residential use in an office area, was the decision, taken in 1960, to give the lower end of Carlton House Terrace to learned societies rather than to the Foreign Office. In return for this self-denying ordinance the government was to enjoy some of the office accommodation to be built on the site of the Mews.

This then was the background to the scheme put forward by the Commissioners in the 1960s for the demolition of the Mews. The pressures were undeniable and understandable — what makes the situation incomprehensible is the fact that public opinion was so deliberately flouted when it could not be circumvented. The Commissioners could not legally be brought within the framework of the normal planning legislation — the L.C.C. could not even make a preservation order without the consent of the Crown Estate Commissioners — and do not seem at any time to have considered whether they had not a greater responsibility than a mere commercial developer to take account of public opinion.

After the western half of the Mews was demolished in 1960, the comprehensive redevelopment seems to have been accepted officially at least, though naïve members of the public continued to protest until the bulldozers moved in in September 1969. Consultations with the Fine Art Commission, the Westminster City Council and the Greater London Council were carried out, planning permission being finally given by the Westminster City Council in July 1967. A scheme brought forward at the last minute to incorporate the Mews in the new building, destined by some philistine touch of irony to house the British Council, was firmly brushed aside as too expensive even to consider once the contract for the £4 million office block had been signed with the developers.

'Perhaps', observed *The Times* on 2 September 1969, 'there would have been no need for delay if the Crown Estates Commission were subject to the normal processes of planning permission and public inquiry. . . . Public awareness of the importance of improving the environment has been steadily increasing. The next step in the preservation of amenity must be the bringing of all public concerns within the scope of the planning system, which was strengthened in the 1968 Town and Country Planning Act.'

The demolition of Carlton Mews, like the case of the Abingdon gasholder, one hopes will lead to changes in the system and be the last disastrous failure of planning of its kind – the real tragedy in the case of Carlton Mews was that it, too, was the last of its kind.

## Adelphi

'In the case of the Adelphi the *commercial* idea is no less grand and full of imagination than is the *artistic* one. The scheme is a fantasia upon antique motifs: the enormous subterranean vaults, the terrace on to the river, and the simple classical houses with their Pompeian decorated pilasters executed in terracotta. . . . But Adelphi was not only a dream of antique architecture; it was just as much a finance-fantasia over risk and profit; the financier was an artist and the artist a financier. . . .' Rassmussen wrote this just before the Adelphi was destroyed – again, as so often, it is the perceptive foreigner who sees the essential and remarkable London, and the natives who acquiesce in its destruction.

The 'Bold Adelphi' scheme was carried out by the brothers Adam between 1768 and 1774, a rash venture only redeemed from financial disaster by a parliamentary lottery. It was, however, ultimately successful, financially as architecturally. The scheme, the largest group of houses by the Adam Brothers, was based upon the building of subterranean arches, at one, two or three levels, which built up the foreshore, as yet unbanked, to the level of the Strand. The massive storage vaults, which stretched 265 feet back to the Strand, were lit by shafts of light from brick arched portholes.

Upon the arches stood Adelphi Terrace, fronting the river, in which the Brothers Adam themselves had a house, No. 4, next to the central house (No. 5) taken by their friend and supporter Garrick. Behind lay John Street, parallel with the river, with Robert and Adam Streets connecting it with Adelphi Terrace.

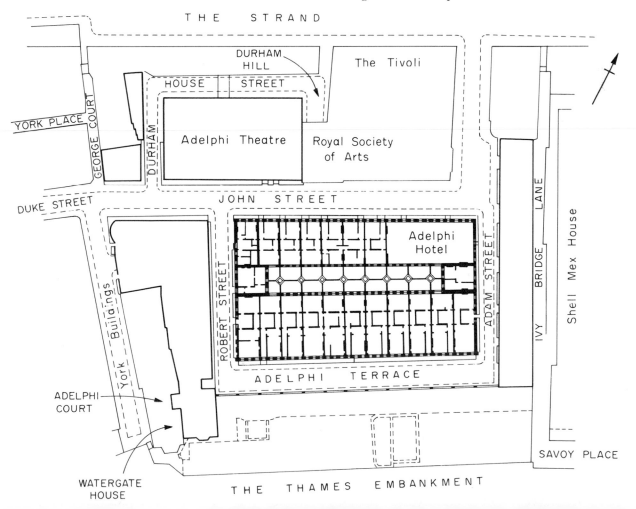

Adelphi Terrace in 1936, just before demolition. The façade was stuccoed over in 1872, when the original leases expired, to bring the building into line with current taste. A heavy pediment was added, the original iron balconies were replaced with Portland stone balusters, and heavy fussy balconies were added to the second floor. The attic windows were enlarged and respectability given to the whole monstrous dress by a heavy Italianate cornice crowned by more Portland stone balustrading. The delicate vertical lines of the original design, emphasized by the pilasters with a honeysuckle design, were swamped.

The drawing-room at No. 4 in the Adams's own house, showing the painted ceiling and elaborate plasterwork, which were used throughout the interiors.

More buildings have disappeared in the City over the last fifty years than anywhere else in London. Many of these were, of course, lost before the war, in the normal course of commercial redevelopment. The war did in fact destroy an estimated third of the City – though only a quarter of its rateable value, a figure which probably reflects the fact that the more modern steel-framed buildings came off better under bombing, and that the high Victorian mansard roofs were particularly vulnerable to incendiaries. Important buildings are listed elsewhere in this book under their individual types, but a great deal of damage was done to lesser buildings, individually insignificant but collectively a loss. One of the things that was lost in the devastated areas was the scale and variety of the nineteenth-century street, particularly in those 'areas of extensive war damage' which were so completely rebuilt.

The City immediately after the war.

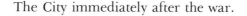

Cheapside has been one of the City's chief commercial streets since mediaeval times, and has of course been rebuilt about once a century. None the less, in 1930 it was a good example of a late Victorian street with the occasional earlier survival.

The south side of Cheapside east of Bread Street in 1931, showing the diversity of modelling and treatment possible with the smaller units of the Victorian street. All the buildings west of St Mary-le-Bow have been rebuilt and the frontage set back.

A photograph showing the street under bombardment in the Blitz in which St Mary-le-Bow has been erased by the war-time censor. Though the interior was a total loss the steeple was never destroyed.

Nos 48 and 49 Cheapside as re-built by R. L. Roumieu in 1874 to replace some timber-framed seventeenth-century buildings. Their unsound condition 'rendered it necessary to rebuild, and the constantly increasing value of space . . . rendered pulling down and rebuilding these premises a prudent and advantageous investment of capital'. Roumieu originally proposed a mediaeval style for both buildings, 'varying in design, but still in unison so as to form one composition'. However, the owners of No. 49 preferred the Renaissance style, thus providing a copybook example of the solution in two different dresses.

Nos 46 and 47 Cheapside, the Georgian warehouse to the west, was totally destroyed by fire in 1881. An altogether more up-to-date solution was provided by Sir Ernest George and Peto, with a cast-iron and red-brick building still mediaeval in flavour with its machicolated chimneys and strong vertical lines but with a regularity and discipline more akin to a modern office block.

Beyond St Mary-le-Bow, at No. 73, an important seventeenth-century house, in which Sir William Turner 'kept his mayoralty' in 1668–9, was demolished in 1929. Despite much alteration, a magnificent staircase remained, and also the fine carving to the attic storey round the original 'Yorkshire' sliding sashes.

This block, at the corner of Queen Street and Cheapside, erected in 1887, presages the modern office block, if one ignores the individual bay windows and the crocheted attic storey, with its lock-up shops below and its independent chambers above. Though extremely common in the City and in such business streets as Holborn at the end of the nineteenth century, it is a type that is rapidly disappearing in favour of higher buildings. It was demolished in 1930.

Bennett's Clock Shop at No. 65 Cheapside, with its figures of Gog and Magog, was one of the best-known of Cheapside frontages. When the shop closed after nearly 200 years, and the building was torn down in 1929, Henry Ford bought the figures for re-erection in his Edison Institute at Greenfield, Michigan.

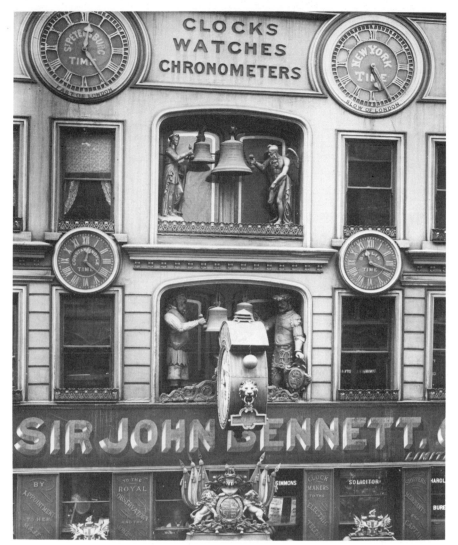

The City is traditionally an area of small sites with no developments on a West End scale. Occasionally, however, comprehensive development of high quality took place on a small estate, usually in a court or cul-de-sac off a main artery.

One such was Catherine Court, Trinity Square, Tower Hill, demolished in 1913 for the new Port of London Authority building. It was a narrow court running between Seething Lane and Trinity Square, with gates across the footway at either end, developed between

1720 and 1725. The long narrow site accommodated four houses fronting on to Seething Lane, and two terraces of narrow houses in the court itself, of which No. 4, on the right at the far end, and No. 5, somewhat advanced of the rest of the north, were double-fronted. It was a particularly serious loss, for there were few courts of this architectural dignity and importance left to show how well this typical feature of City town-planning (*left*) could be handled.

St Helen's Place, off Bishopsgate, in 1911 (*below*), developed by the Leathersellers' Company about 1800. The whole street was demolished and redeveloped in 1912.

# Cloth Fair, Smithfield

Cloth Fair was an enclave behind St Bartholomew-the-Great, and was full in 1870, in Augustus Hare's words, of 'old though squalid houses of Elizabethan and Jacobin date'. Though many of these had in fact probably been repaired and reconstructed, the mediaeval street pattern survived here, as nowhere else in the City, until 1900, when it was irreparably damaged by slum clearance. The old houses backing on to the churchyard, built largely of wood, with over-hanging storeys and arranged round a series of closed courts, were inhabited by old-clothes merchants and rag-and-bone dealers, presenting a considerable public health problem.

Churchyard of St Bartholomew-the-Great, 1877.

Cloth Fair looking east about 1905. At the end on the left was the Dick Whittington public house, which claimed to be the oldest pub in London. This was probably not true as it only became a beerhouse in 1848, though it was a seventeenth-century house. Along with three other of the six pubs there in 1870, it has disappeared.

The western gateway of Cloth Fair demolished about 1905 by the L.C.C. The houses on the left backed on to the churchyard and were demolished, despite remonstrations by antiquarians, about 1915.

Westminster Law Courts.

# IV
# PUBLIC BUILDINGS

## Government Buildings

The late nineteenth century saw an enormous increase in the administrative duties of both the central and local authorities. The legal and administrative reforms of the period made necessary the expansion of the civil service which has continued into our own day. This has led to the demolition of many older buildings to make room for new government offices, notably in Whitehall. Legal buildings were among the first purpose-built government offices – administration continued from converted premises for much longer.

John Soane (1753–1837) was not only Architect to the Bank of England (1788–1833) but from 1790 he held government offices of gradually increasing importance, culminating in his appointment, 1814–32, as an 'Attached Architect' to the Office of Works. It is tragic how little of his work in London has survived intact from these two major appointments. The State Paper Office was demolished for the building of the Foreign Office in 1868, while Barry remodelled much of his Privy Council and Board of Trade offices in the 1840s.

His INSOLVENT DEBTORS' COURT in Portugal Street in 1911, before demolition for the building of the Land Registry.

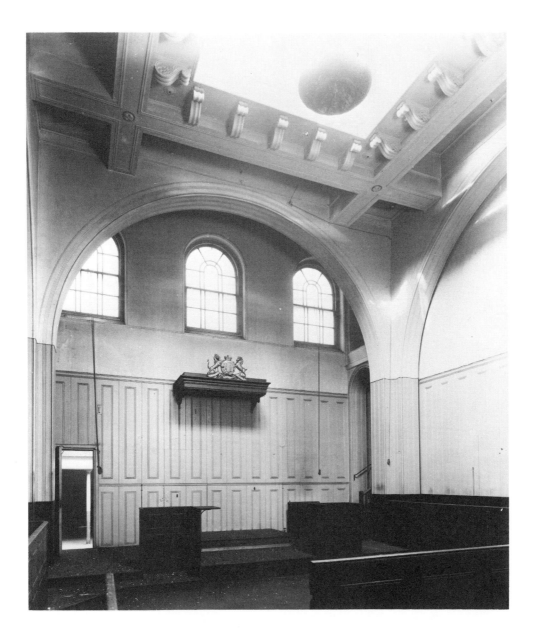

A building which demonstrates both his characteristic ingenuity and his affection for and brilliant handling of top-lit spaces was the WESTMINSTER LAW COURTS, demolished in 1883 after the Strand Courts were built. The main façade had been begun by William Kent, and extended in a haphazard fashion, and Soane was asked to extend the façade on to St Margaret Street, now part of Parliament Square, and to fit five new courts between Kent's façade and Westminster Hall itself. Despite Soane's preference for a classical style to contrast with the mediaeval hall, he was forced by the Commons to use Gothic. Fortunately, within the building he was allowed to use the classical style in which he had already carried out the Bank of England. Though each court was identical in plan, each rectangular space was varied by being given a different spaced gallery or lantern. (See also page 107.)

Court of Exchequer.

Soane's Gothic addition to New Palace Yard.

THE GENERAL POST OFFICE started business in converted premises in 1688. In 1824–9 Sir Robert Smirke designed and built the first Post Office headquarters on the east side of St Martin's-le-Grand. The original building was extended by putting a further two storeys on top, and extending the basement by putting roof lights in place of the paved courtyard. Other premises were built to the north and to the west of St Martin's Lane, but these expedients proved inadequate. In 1903–10, a new Post Office was built further west on the site of part of Christ's Hospital, and the old Post Office was demolished in three months in 1912.

THE ROLLS CHAPEL was originally built to serve a house for converted Jews set up by Henry III. It was rebuilt about 1617 to the design of Inigo Jones. It later became part of the official residence of the Keeper of the Rolls, and the records of the Court of Chancery were kept there till the building of the Public Record Office, begun in 1856–70, and finished in 1896–7. Despite its undoubted antiquity, little effort was made to save it, the plea being put forward that it was in poor condition, always a suspect claim, and particularly reprehensible when it is made by a government department about a building which has been in its own charge for a number of years. Together with the Rolls Office, built in 1717–24, it was demolished in 1896–7, despite the objections of the Society for the Protection of Ancient Buildings, who pointed out that the Chapel was 'a more reliable record, a more living document of antiquity, than the papers for the mere storage of which it is proposed to destroy it. . . .'

## Local Authority Buildings

With the rapid and still continuing change in the government of London over the last hundred years, there has been a corresponding change in the location and style of the offices from which its administration was carried on. The earliest administrative units were the parish vestries abolished under the Metropolitan Management Act of 1855, which set up the Metropolitan Board of Works, which gave way in its turn to the London County Council in 1888.

The L.C.C. gradually absorbed a number of independent bodies which were responsible for such matters as workhouse accommodation, public health and education. The building of County Hall on the South Bank after 1906 led to the physical amalgamation of the offices and the demolition of outlying property.

The VESTRY HALL, CLERKENWELL, originally the Watchhouse, in which the Commissioners for Paving, Watching, etc., met from 1814 onwards, and which was converted into the Vestry room for the new Borough set up under the Metropolitan Management Act. Designed by W. P. Griffiths, a local antiquarian architect, best known for his restoration of St John's Gate, it was typical of the unpretentious buildings in which London's government was carried on in the early Victorian period, and which were succeeded by the more flamboyant Town Halls, built for the Metropolitan Boroughs created by the local government acts of 1888 and 1899. The Vestry Hall remained in use till the building of Finsbury Town Hall in 1892.

LAMBETH PARISH WATCHHOUSE (built 1825), in Lambeth High Street in 1912, apparently demolished between the wars. There was a second Lambeth Watchhouse next to St John's Church in the Waterloo Road, which existed till 1930. Not all the watchhouses were as solid as this; some were of wood, and there is an account of one watchman, watchhouse and all, being heaved over the wall into Bunhill Fields cemetery by an active band of ruffians. The general ineffectiveness of the parish watchmen led to their supersession by the Metropolitan Police under the Police Act of 1829.

# Guildhall

First amongst the City halls in both time and importance is, of course, Guildhall itself, where in earlier times the companies were content to meet, and from which the government of the City has been carried on for over five hundred years. During this period it has suffered a good deal of damage, and almost more well-meaning 'restoration'. After the Great Fire it stood open to the sky, with blackened walls and a structure so damaged that Wren had to fill the western crypt with temporary arches that still hold up the floor of Guildhall today. His flat plaster ceiling in the classical manner was much disapproved of by Sir Horace Jones, the City Architect, and replaced by a fine hammer-beam roof in 1861. Jones's roof and interior were burnt out in 1940, in the same 'Fire Raid' which destroyed the seventeenth-century Aldermen's Court Room and the Victorian Council Chamber. Guildhall has since been extensively repaired, but drastic changes are proposed by the City authorities for the surrounding area.

The original proposal put forward in 1953, and supported at a Public Inquiry by representatives of the Ministry of Public Building and Works, was that, the Guildhall being 'the most notable and impressive piece of mediaeval architecture in the Kingdom', all later accretions and buildings round the hall should be demolished. This clearance would also assist in the circulation problem presented by the large cars of important visitors to the Guildhall on official occasions. Included in the demolitions were to be the remains of the bombed Art Gallery, on the right, and Dance's Guildhall Justice Room, on the left. In an access of enthusiasm for mediaeval purity as single-minded and heavy-handed as any of the Great Victorian restorers, the City also planned to demolish the curious 'Gothick' façade designed by Dance in 1789, and inspired, we are told, by Indian temples. Fortunately, but only through the intervention of the Georgian Group, the City was prevented from tearing off the Dance front, though his Justice Room was demolished in 1969. They have, however, destroyed the intimate quality of Guildhall Yard, more mediaeval perhaps, in its heterogeneous collection of buildings round a closed space, than the restored Guildhall with its turning circle for limousines will be. With a certain inconsistency the mediaeval parts of Guildhall are to be masked by a modern ambulatory which pierces the fifteenth-century porch. The City Architect's concern for Guildhall's mediaeval parts was pinpointed by a complaint from the historical experts of the Ministry of Housing that two mediaeval staircases had been filled in with concrete, as part of the restoration of the mediaeval eastern crypt. The City Corporation's reply that the staircases were filled in on the advice of the Ministry of Works merely underlined the ridiculous situation which prevailed in the field of government experts, where ancient monuments were dealt with by the Ministry of Works, and historic buildings by the Ministry of Housing. These experts are not yet united in one department at the Department of the Environment.

The Guildhall about 1890, showing the Justice Room on the left designed by George Dance the Younger, Clerk of the City Works. The east side of Dance's Gothick front was torn down in the 1870s but restored in 1909. Behind can be seen Jones's high roof with its 'mediaeval' lantern and dormers. On the right the Art Gallery, opened 1886, in the buildings originally designed in 1823 as Law Courts, by William Mountague.

The Aldermen's Court Room, by Wren, destroyed in 1940.

Sir Horace Jones's Council Chamber of 1884.

## City Halls

Though there are eighty-two City companies, not all have had halls, and by the nineteenth century only about half the companies still had halls. By this period most of the companies had lost their connection with the trades they represented, and had become little more than friendly societies. Their considerable wealth, however, led over half of those that survived to rebuild their halls. Some companies let their halls for commercial purposes, others demolished them and sold the site. Only the Ironmongers' Hall was destroyed in 1917, but in the Second World War, of the thirty-six halls then standing, eighteen were destroyed, fifteen more or less severely damaged, leaving only three intact. The Merchant Taylors' Hall in Threadneedle Street was a particularly serious loss, as it was the only hall to preserve anything of its mediaeval buildings.

A unique hall completely destroyed in the Second World War was the BARBER SURGEONS' HALL in Monkwell Street, dating from 1634, which survived the Great Fire. The elegant small courtroom with its polygonal lantern was attributed to Inigo Jones, who also built an elliptical theatre for the Company, later demolished.

THE BREWERS' HALL in Addle Street, very little altered since it was rebuilt in 1673, described in 1917 as 'a building of singular charm and interest, and better than any other among . . . since it is almost untouched by the hand of a restorer. . . .' The quadrangle in 1939, the porthole windows on the left giving on to the court-room. *Right,* The quadrangle in 1941.

THE CLOTHWORKERS' HALL in 1940, by Samuel Angell, a fellow pupil of Philip Hardwick, architect of the Gold-smiths' Hall, and working in the same confident High Victorian classical tradition. It was opened by the Prince Consort himself in 1860. The Hall, in Mincing Lane, was destroyed in 1940.

THE CURRIERS' HALL of 1874 by John Belcher, rebuilt twice in three years when a commercial firm wished the Company to move its newly built frontage. Though only twenty years later than the Clothworkers' Hall Belcher's design was in the Arts and Crafts idiom, reflecting the interest in the mediaeval guild halls from which the livery halls derived. The hall, fronting on to London Wall, was sold in 1920, and was destroyed in the Second World War.

THE TEMPLE OF FREEMASONS' HALL behind the Freemason's Tavern, Nos 57–8 Great Queen Street, about 1900. The Temple was built in 1775, and was the most important executed work of Thomas Sandby (1721–98). The Temple was preserved in the extensive rebuilding of 1864–5, but was demolished in 1932, when the Connaught Rooms were rebuilt on the site.

# Legal Inns

'Opening off from Chancery Lane are various other lanes, quiet dingy nooks, some of them in the guise of streets going no whither, and others existing as the entrances to so-called Inns of Court, Inns of which all knowledge has for years been lost to the outer world of the laity, and as I believe, lost almost equally to the inner world of the legal profession. Who has ever heard of Symond's Inn? Of Staples' Inn, who knows the purpose or use? Who are its members, and what do they do as such?'

Anthony Trollope writing in the 1860s thus summarised the defunct condition of these minor inns, of which were were originally a large number. Half of one is all that now remains, and that so heavily restored that it is difficult to recognise it as an ancient building. Mostly mediaeval in origin, many of them were rebuilt as chambers rather than collegiate buildings in the eighteenth and nineteenth centuries. Furnival's Inn in Holborn, for instance, was rebuilt by the builder Peto in 1818, as chambers and a hotel, before being demolished in 1895 for the Prudential Assurance building. Lyon's Inn was demolished in 1863, Symond's Inn in 1873, for the erection of offices and chambers at No. 22 Chancery Lane. The buildings were often corporately owned by a handful of 'ancients' and a few junior members, as in the case of Serjeants' Inn. The legal rank of serjeant was terminated under the Judicature Act, 1873, and the remaining members dissolved their Inn and sold it in 1877, dividing the proceeds of £57,000 among them, a procedure said to have caused 'much comment'. Collectively the loss of so many groups of seventeenth-century buildings, each with their gardens and courts, was very great, and radically altered the legal hinterland between Fleet Street and Holborn.

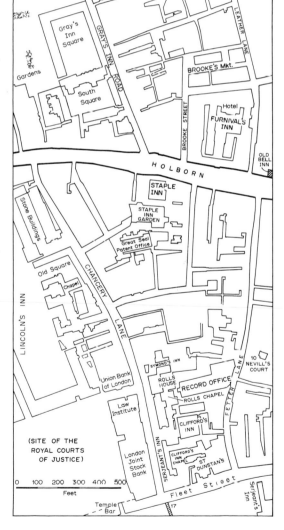

*Sketch map of the Legal Inns c. 1870. Buildings discussed in the text appear in bold. For the Inns to the west of the Royal Courts of Justice see page 73.*

CLEMENT'S INN, partially demolished in 1868 for the Law Courts, was finally pulled down in 1893. It was attached to the Inner Temple, and was particularly renowned for the Garden House, and the sun-dial sold by the Ancients in 1884 for 20 guineas.

CLIFFORD'S INN survived the longest, being demolished in 1935. The 'Rules' or senior members inspired by the Serjeants' example, sold their Inn in 1903, but were forced to disgorge the proceeds for legal education. Clifford's Inn was bought by William Willett, the builder, for £100,000; his schemes did not mature, and the Inn remained as chambers until 1935 when it was demolished for the erection of a very banal block of flats.

NEW INN stood across the line of Aldwych, and disappeared in the Strand Improvement Scheme of 1900.

Although little more than a collection of chambers, it still possessed a very fine Hall.

# London Clubs

The club succeeded the coffee house as the meeting place of the well-to-do Londoner. 'A younger son', wrote a German visitor in 1853, 'cannot live and do as others do, within the limits of his income. . . . The club is his home, and stands him in the place of an establishment. At the club, spacious and splendidly furnished saloons are at his disposal; there is a library, a reading-room, baths and dressing-rooms. . . . He finds all the last new works and periodicals; a crowd of servants attend upon him and the cooking is irreproachable. . . . Lordly halls, splendid carpets, sofas, arm-chairs, strong, soft and roomy, in which a man might dream away his life; writing and reading rooms tranquil enough to suit a poet, and yet grand, imposing, aristocratic; doors covered with cloth to prevent the noise of their opening and shutting and their brass handles resplendent as the purest gold; enormous fireplaces surrounded by slabs of the whitest marble; the furniture of mahogany and palisander; the staircases broad and imposing as in the palazzos of Rome; the kitchens *chefs d'œuvres* of modern architecture. . . .' (Schlesinger: *Saunterings in and around London,* 1853.)

These were, of course the 'senior' clubs, whose waiting lists were not yet so long as to create the fashion for 'junior' clubs, most of whom were founded in the 1860s and 1870s. On the whole it is among the 'junior' clubs that the casualties have occurred. First waiting lists and then membership have shrunk as upper-middle-class Englishmen have taken to working harder and marrying younger – both practices inimical to club life. Eighty clubs listed in a directory of 1879 had swelled to over 150 by 1914, and since 1945 a number have disappeared or have moved to smaller premises, reducing the number to about 80. There is a great temptation for a diminishing number of members occupying a large and expensive building on a valuable site — rebuilding could give them smaller, more economic premises as part of a new office block, and even total disappearance of their club would be compensated for by enormous financial benefits.

Four clubs of the golden age have gone – the Oriental Club, the Carlton, the Army and Navy, and the City of London. The Junior Carlton, the Guards, erected 1858 by H. Harrison, and the Junior United Service, of the later generation, have been demolished. There were others of course, 'converted' clubhouses as well, including those of the Turf Club, No. 85 Piccadilly, the Isthmian Club at No. 105 (formerly Hertford House) and Savile Club (demolished 1934), at No. 107 Piccadilly, or the Royal Thames Yacht Club, in a Cubitt mansion in Knightsbridge, demolished in 1961–3.

THE ARMY AND NAVY CLUB on the corner of St James's Square and Pall Mall, built to the design of C. O. Parnell and Alfred Smith in 1848–51. This lithograph by Smith shows the staircase, a feature essential to give a club entrance the proper importance, but a space-wasting one which may well have contributed to its disappearance. Behind the stairs is the morning room, and on the left the coffee-room. In 1959 the Club were granted permission to demolish and rebuild on the grounds that the original part of the Club was obsolete and difficult to run. Despite the vigorous opposition of the Victorian Society this was permitted.

THE CARLTON (*overleaf*) was, of course, the most important High Tory club, and indeed the first political club as such. The clubhouse was rebuilt to the design of Basevi (who died before work started) and Sydney Smirke in 1854–6. Smirke followed Barry in adopting the palazzo style, this time an adaptation of the Libreria di San Marco in Venice. Unfortunately Smirke made the error of choosing Caen stone. Decay began ten years after the building was begun, and continued until it was refaced by Blomfield in 1923–4. The Club was bombed in October 1940.

THE ORIENTAL CLUB (*below*), No. 18 Hanover Square, founded in 1824 by a group of officers employed by the East India Company, and therefore ineligible for the military clubs in Pall Mall. They took the advice of that most famous of 'Indian' officers, the Duke of Wellington, to make sure that the Club was freehold. It was, and when an extremely good offer was made in 1962, the Committee thought it right to accept, particularly in view of the parlous state in which so many clubs found themselves.

The Drawing-room of 1827–8, by Benjamin Dean Wyatt and Philip Wyatt, the architects of Londonderry House.

THE JUNIOR CARLTON between Pall Mall and St James's Square, founded in 1864 to accommodate the large number of keen Conservatives on the waiting list of the Carlton. By 1866, the Club had commissioned David Brandon to design a clubhouse, extended in 1885–6 by J. Macvicar Anderson, a further two bays to the west. In 1963 the Club was given permission to demolish and rebuild as part of a modern office block.

The enormous coffee room, as the main dining-room of a club is usually called, considerably extended and redecorated by Macvicar Anderson in 1885, looking from the original strangers' coffee room through into the members' portion

Philip Hardwick's CITY OF LONDON CLUB (1833–4) is the only clubhouse in the City, and will soon be demolished.

The double cube dining-room is particularly interesting, both for its fine proportions and for the Venetian windows. These seem to be a further development from those of Taylor at the Bank of England, and foreshadow those designed by Hardwick for his unexecuted Euston Great Hall.

Its loss is a sad tale of a fine building falling through one gaping rent in the planning laws after another. In the first place, it was quite unaccountably left off the list of buildings of architectural and historic importance when the City was originally listed. In 1963, the L.C.C. spotlisted it and the National Provincial Bank in Bishopsgate, when they were both threatened by the same monster redevelopment. At the public inquiry the Ministry inspector refused to list either building, but the then Minister, Sir Keith Joseph, to his credit saved Gibson's Bank, but though expressing sympathy with admirers of the Club, refused to save it on the grounds that to do so would be to make the redevelopment more difficult, and gave outline planning permission. In 1969, when detailed plans were put forward, the G.L.C. made a further effort to save the Club by spotlisting it, on the grounds that the new 1968 planning legislation gave them power to do so without incurring the punitive compensation which has effectively prevented the saving of any major building in London since 1948. The City opposed this proposal, as throughout it had been in favour of the demolition of the Club, and the Ministry refused to make an issue of this important test case for the new legislation on which so many hopes had been pinned by those interested in the preservation of London.

Despite the urging of the Victorian Society and the G.L.C.'s experts on the value of the building, Lord Kennet, then Minister, took the line that despite the new legislation in the meanwhile, it would be improper to reverse a predecessor's planning permission, particularly when a good deal of time and money had been put into the plans.

The implications of this decision are almost more grave than the loss of the Club, and it is a sad comment on the City's priorities that the Club, which has the most distinguished membership of any club in the City, has sold its historic and unique clubhouse without apparent regret.

More closures and amalgamations are inevitable among West End clubs – one secretary is reported to have forecast a fifty per cent casualty list over the next five years, while others may be tempted to redevelop their clubhouse on the same basis as the Army and Navy and Junior Carlton clubs have done. Amongst those in some difficulty, it is rumoured, are the United University Club, with a clubhouse by Blomfield (1906), the National Liberal, whose Doulton extravaganza by Waterhouse (1884) survived a direct hit in the war and should be preserved from the house-breaker, and the East India and Sports Club in St James's Square which is reputed to be seeking another club with which to amalgamate, while the Oxford and Cambridge has decided to disband.

THE OXFORD AND CAMBRIDGE CLUB. The North Library with its original bookshelves, typical of the simple dignified Grecian style throughout the building. The clubhouse was designed by Sir Robert Smirke and his son Sydney in 1835–8.

# Museums

THE MUSEUM OF PRACTICAL GEOLOGY in Jermyn Street, one of the first great national British museums, established through the influence of Sir Henry de la Bèche, designed by James Pennethorne, the Crown Architect, and opened by the Prince Consort in May 1851. It housed the Geological Survey and a staff of geologists and students, as well as such exhibits as the collection of stone samples, made for the construction of the new Houses of Parliament. It soon outgrew its site, but though its removal to join the South Kensington complex was long discussed this did not occur till 1934. Pennethorne's fine building was demolished in 1936.

The Upper Exhibition Gallery, showing Pennethorne's superb handling of structural cast iron, still to be admired at the Public Record Office and the Patent Office.

THE CRYSTAL PALACE, at Sydenham, in 1928. Sir Joseph Paxton's masterpiece of iron and glass was moved to Sydenham after the Great Exhibition closed in 1852, and became the centrepiece of a great amusement park, both improving and recreational. Paxton's original building was extended from 1851 feet to 2756 by the addition of transepts at either end, and it was heightened by a further 44 feet. The interior was divided into courts filled with cultural exhibits. On the terraces outside were magnificent fountains, supplied with sufficient water by the two 300-foot water towers, and a collection of statuary. On the night of 30 November 1936, the Crystal Palace caught fire and was totally burnt out.

The Mediaeval Court in 1860.

THE ARCHITECTURAL MUSEUM housed a very important collection of architectural models and plaster casts, inspired by the 1851 Exhibition, and the general enthusiasm for Gothic. It included casts from all sources, including some made from Venetian buildings for Ruskin himself, and a great number given by practising architects, who had them made when restoring old buildings. Occasionally, damaged mediaeval work which had been totally replaced was also presented. The Museum, at 18 Tufton Street, was designed by George Somers Clarke and Ewan Christian in 1869, and became the first home of the Architectural Association. When the latter moved to Bloomsbury, the collection went back to the Victoria and Albert Museum at South Kensington, and the building was sold to the National School for the Blind and rebuilt about 1935.

It is very unfortunate that the collection appears to have been broken up as intact it would have been an invaluable record of Victorian taste and enthusiasm.

There have been, of course, an enormous number of galleries built in London, many being converted from other uses. Some of them were mere commercial enterprises; others, like John Boydell's unsuccessful Shakespeare Gallery in Pall Mall, had far loftier aims. One of the best known of the commercial galleries was the Egyptian Hall at Nos 170–1 Piccadilly, built by William Bullock in 1811–12 to the design of P. F. Robinson. This was the first building to be designed in London in the 'Egyptian' style, and struck a very exotic note amongst the conventional Georgian houses of Piccadilly. Though considerably altered internally, the EGYPTIAN HALL remained an exhibition centre until its demolition in 1905. As one of the earliest showplaces for animated pictures in London, it set the architectural style for a number of purpose-built cinemas.

The private gallery was a feature of large eighteenth- and nineteenth-century houses, and most of them have been mentioned in connection with the mansions to which they belonged. It is not a solecism to refer to them as public buildings, for many private collections were open to selected members of the public through the generosity – and love of display – of their rich and noble owners. Nineteenth-century guidebooks are full of instructions as to how to obtain tickets to such really fantastic collections as that of Devonshire or Grosvenor House.

Possibly the most remarkable private collection in both history and extent was that of the Earl of Ellesmere, great-nephew and heir of the Duke of Bridgewater, who made his money in building canals and invested some of it in the purchase of the Orleans collection of works of art. Lord Ellesmere employed Barry to build Bridgewater House, which is happily still standing, but the great gallery was destroyed by a bomb in 1940 (*right*). The gallery was in Barry's most magnificent classical style (*below*).

One of the most unusual private galleries was the summer house in Buckingham Palace gardens (1845) designed by Edward Blore, and intended as a trial for the artists who were to paint frescoes for the walls of the new Houses of Parliament. Prince Albert and his 'adviser in art', Ludwig Gruner, were largely responsible and Gruner published a coloured book on the pavilion in 1846. The central octagonal room was illustrated by eight different artists, including Eastlake, Landseer, Maclise and Etty, all painting subjects from *Comus*. The two side rooms were decorated respectively in the Pompeian manner, and with subjects taken from Scott, chosen because they were felt to be the most classical and most romantic of subjects respectively. The pavilion was demolished in 1928 because it was felt to be too dilapidated to preserve.

THE IMPERIAL INSTITUTE in South Kensington was founded after the Imperial Exhibition of 1886, and the building was erected between 1887 and 1893 to the designs of T. E. Collcutt. Under proposals for the expansion of the Imperial College of Science put forward in 1955, the Institute and other buildings on the site between Queen's Gate and Exhibition Road, north of Imperial Institute Road, were to be demolished. This was made necessary by the desire to contain Imperial College within the site, and to rehouse the Imperial Institute on the same site, though not in its historic building, and to respect a gentleman's agreement that the Royal College of Music should not be disturbed in its ugly and undistinguished premises. The Fine Art Commission remonstrated that 'the scheme . . . did not seem to pay enough regard to the importance, architecturally and historically, to London of some of the existing buildings of the site, particularly the main block of the Institute, and No. 170 Queen's Gate [by Norman Shaw]'. It was suggested that the latter building might be used to house the science library even if it were not appropriate for teaching purposes. 'The

Victorian grandeur of the Institute would provide a valuable foil to the new buildings and would also contribute a sense of historical continuity appropriate to a collegiate group.' The Commission also suggested that the College's expressed intention to confine its teaching premises to this site, which was said to necessitate the demolition, might have to be reassessed and then the Government would be criticised for having allowed the unnecessary destruction of such an important building.

The publication of the Commission's report produced a considerable storm of informed protest – predictably John Betjeman and H. S. Goodhart Rendel were on the side of the Institute, but less convinced 'Victorians' like Sir Hugh Casson, Professor A. E. Richardson and Sir Julian Huxley also raised their voices in protest, among many other complainants, one of whom enquired pertinently in a letter to *The Times*:

'And what of the Fine Art Commission? If its recommendations are to be ignored by the authority which set it up can it be held to serve any useful purpose?'

The University of London, having already destroyed so much more of Bloomsbury, was unmoved by the public outcry, which the principal, Dr D. W. Logan, dismissed as 'stoked up'. Fortunately, however, the pressure of public opinion saved the central tower, which the architects were instructed to incorporate into the new scheme, though the rest of the Institute building was demolished.

Private literary institutions were a feature of nineteenth-century London, many of which have perished. One of the oldest was the LONDON INSTITUTION itself, founded in 1805, and housed in a fine building of 1819 in Finsbury Circus, by William Brooks, demolished in 1936.

THE ROYAL SOCIETY OF MUSICIANS, Nos 11–13 Lisle Street, Leicester Square, built in 1808 to the design of Thomas Hopper (1776–1856). The building was demolished in 1931 for the extension of the Gerrard Street Telephone Exchange.
The Boardroom just before demolition, drawn by Hanslip Fletcher, who has recorded so many of London's vanished landmarks.

THE INSTITUTION OF CIVIL ENGINEERS in Great George Street in 1896. This building, designed by the younger Charles Barry, survived only a few years. It was demolished for the new Local Government building in 1910. The Institution was re-housed on the opposite side of the street at No. 8.

135

# Schools

Amongst institutions, schools are peculiarly, and rightly, vulnerable to change, as curricula change and teaching methods alter. Sometimes, as in so many architectural and intellectual fashions, the wheel comes full circle and, the large Victorian schoolrooms having been laboriously partitioned off in the last half-century, open-plan classrooms are now again the vogue.

Two particular trends have led to the demolition of school buildings. Firstly, there is the general trend for all residential institutions to move outwards into cheaper and healthier suburban surroundings, which has affected almost all London boarding schools, so that Westminster alone remains in the centre. Secondly, there have been enormous improvements in the state system leading to great advances in the buildings, first from the little parish schools to the great Victorian 'three-decker' Board Schools which dominated the areas of working-class housing which they served. Now these leviathans are being demolished in favour of lower, more easily run buildings with more specialised classrooms.

ST GEORGE'S SCHOOLS, Battersea Park, designed by Joseph Peacock in 1857, when the area was being laid out. It was a forerunner of the three-decker, accommodating 200 boys, 150 girls and 150 infants in separate schools, and also three residences for teachers. It closed in 1969, when a new school was built.

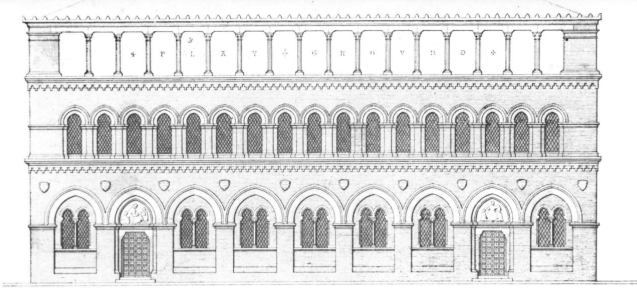

ST MARTIN-IN-THE-FIELDS' NORTHERN SCHOOLS,
Castle Street, designed in 1849 by J. W. Wild (1814–92), remarkable more for its architectural than educational innovation. It was
welcomed for its use of cut and moulded brick, for its urban
appearance, as well as for its pioneering use of the Italian Gothic
style, a use warmly commended by G. E. Street, who pointed out
that it would be easy to adapt to commercial buildings, fitting shop
fronts into the ground floor arcade. As school architecture, it is also
interesting for the roof-top playground, an early form of this solution to the problem of a cramped site. It ceased to be a school in
1939 and was demolished in 1955.

THE CITY OF LONDON SCHOOL, Honey Lane, Cheapside,
erected in 1837 to the design of J. B. Bunning, in a romantic Gothic
more generally used for rural schools. The school was so successful
that in 1882 it was moved to the newly made Victoria Embankment
and Bunning's buildings were demolished.

A great number of City companies support schools, of which the most famous is St Paul's, controlled by the Mercers' Company. That Company had its own school, finally closed in 1958, as did the Merchant Taylors, whose school has survived several moves.

MERCHANT TAYLORS' SCHOOL was established in Suffolk Lane, before the Great Fire, and the school was rebuilt there and remained till 1875, when it moved to a new school on the former Charterhouse site, designed by Edward I'Anson, an old boy. In 1933, the school moved out of London, and I'Anson's buildings were sold to St Bartholomew's Hospital.

ST PAUL'S SCHOOL in 1963. The school moved to Hammersmith from St Paul's Churchyard in 1884, into one of Waterhouse's characteristic red-brick piles, heavy in outline, and indigestible in the carbolic red of its material, which obstinately refused to weather. None the less, it was a great loss to the neighbourhood when it was demolished in 1968, on the school's removal to Barnes.

CHRIST'S HOSPITAL, founded by Edward VI on the site of the Greyfriars Monastery at Newgate, and rebuilt after the Fire to the design of Wren. Despite very considerable opposition, a Royal Commission reported in 1890 that 'for a thorough reform in the management and discipline of Christ's Hospital, its removal from London is indispensable'. This recommendation was carried out in 1902, and, again despite the opposition of almost all London antiquarians and such early amenity pressure groups as the Society for the Protection of Ancient Buildings, the Metropolitan Public Gardens Association and the National Trust, the whole five-acre site was cleared and sold to the Post Office. In the words of Philip Norman, a leading antiquarian and an important member of the London Survey Committee: 'One knows the enormous monetary value of land in London, and that the authorities of Christ's Hospital were bound to do the best they could on behalf of the young generation'. None the less, he regarded the 'sale and clearance of the land as the heaviest blow that has been dealt to lovers of old London for many years' (*London Vanished and Vanishing*).

'A bird's-eye view of Christ's Hospital' from the tower of Christ Church Newgate, showing on the lower left Wren's old building incorporating the Greyfriars' cloisters, top left the Hall (1825–9), and top right the Mathematical and Grammar School (1832) by John Shaw, Surveyor to the Hospital. In the centre is the old hall, again above original cloisters, and the 'Grecian cloisters' of 1836, re-erected at Horsham.

Shaw's Hall, reputed to be the largest unsupported span in London after Westminster Hall.

The Courtroom.

These photographs were taken by the L.C.C., who even then were very much aware of the need to record disappearing buildings.

Equally tragic was the loss of the FOUNDLING HOSPITAL in Bloomsbury and the more deplorable because by 1926 public opinion had been awakened to the quickening pace of destruction in London. There was even a proposal that the University of London should make its headquarters in the Foundling Hospital complex rather than in western Bloomsbury on the Bedford Estate. It was doubly unfortunate that this was not adopted, since this might have preserved not only the fine Hospital buildings but also much of residential Bloomsbury. In a percipient article which anticipated the public indignation, but not perhaps the public impotence, over the destruction of Woburn Square fifty years later, the writer of an article in *Country Life* suggested that it was hardly likely that during 'this house famine Londoners would stand up indifferently and watch the demolition of a considerable number of homes'.

'It is difficult to understand', he concluded, 'how any public body which has at heart the interests of education and the welfare of London generally can have any doubt as to which is the better of the two sites. The well-placed island site of the Foundling Hospital with its spacious grounds and fine timber, its ready access to the great North London termini, with a tube station and route of tramways practically on the site together with substantial buildings which can easily be adapted for administrative office, examination rooms and classrooms. . . .'

In the event, three-quarters of the site was preserved as open space by a private group headed by Lord Rothermere.

The Hospital was started in 1739 by Captain Coram, to provide for abandoned infants. The buildings were erected between 1749 and 1752 to the design of Theodore Jacobsen.

The Chapel, demolished with the rest of the buildings in 1928, with its original high box pews and fine plasterwork. The choir here was renowned, and it was here that Handel performed his *Messiah* in aid of Hospital funds.

## Almshouses

The almshouse was the successor to the mediaeval hospital, often a collegiate foundation which cared for the old and indigent, sometimes combining it with another community service like education. This composite nature survived in many post-mediaeval foundations – Sion College, for instance, was both college and almshouse – until separated by the Charity Commissioners in the nineteenth century.

London boasted an enormous number of almshouses – Weale, in his guidebook of 1851, listed 110 foundations, from substantial and well-managed foundations, like Morden College, to tiny foundations, like Nicholas Butler's almshouses in Westminster for two poor men and their wives. There were also a large number of parish almshouses. By the nineteenth century they were often in the wrong place, the former suburb had become noisy and central, and the trustees were often short of money to repair old buildings sitting on sites whose value was out of proportion to the use to which they were put. Many institutions were moved out early in the century, but the Charity Commissioners only produced a number of their schemes for re-organisation after 1870, and the following three decades saw the disappearance of a very large number of these quasi-collegiate groups of buildings, in favour either of amalgamation and rebuilding, or of the substitution of pensions for a dwelling. Many of them were only cottages, but others were interesting groups of buildings, valuable as an architectural group, and even more, in the words of one protesting contemporary, as 'a quiet little oasis, as a stretch of breathing space among a crowded population'. These were eliminated to provide money for schools and suburban homes for the inmates, entirely correctly in contemporary terms, but with a corresponding loss in the diversity of fabric of Central London, and therefore in the lives of Londoners generally. It was, however, a period during which antiquarian protest was becoming more effective, and some major groups, like the Trinity Hospital in the Mile End Road (1695), and the Ironmongers' Almshouses, now the Geffrye Museum, in the Kingsland Road, were saved through public protest.

JUDD'S ALMSHOUSES, Great St Helen's, demolished about 1892 by the Skinners' Company to whom they belonged, together with a larger foundation in the Mile End Road. Suburban almshouses were built from the proceeds. Many other company almshouses went about the same time.

Westminster was a typical area of Outer London, with a large number of charitable foundations, whose removal had an enormous cumulative effect. The four involved in this amalgamation, Emmanuel Hospital, founded by Lady Dacre in 1594, St Margaret's or the Greencoat School (1633), Palmer's of 1654, and Emery Hill's, founded early in the eighteenth century, have all vanished. The scholastic endowments were removed in 1873, Emery Hill's Almshouses were rebuilt to house the inmates of Palmer's and Butler's, and the sites of the others sold. Emmanuel Hospital, the largest and most important architecturally, was demolished against the advice of the Charity Commissioners, and in the teeth of considerable public opposition which went as far as the High Court. The Trustees of Emmanuel Hospital, the Lord Mayor and Aldermen of the City of London, first announced their intention of demolishing the almshouse in 1889, but were only allowed to do so after a three-year battle, in 1892.

*Sketch map to show the Westminster Almshouses c. 1870.*

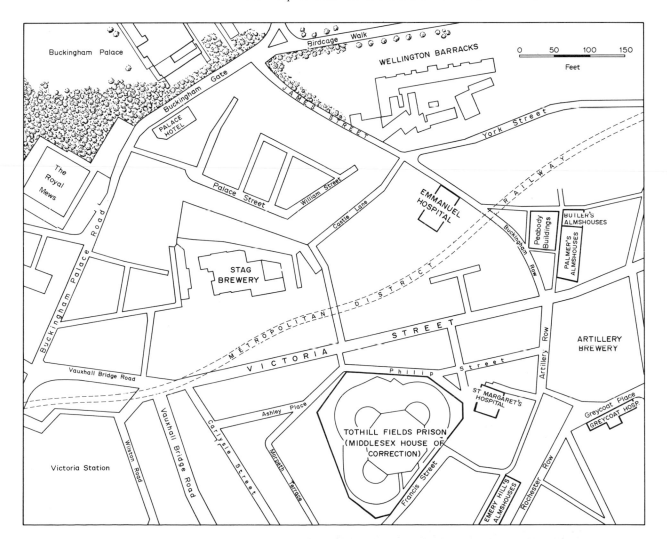

EMMANUEL HOSPITAL in 1886. It was rebuilt in Queen Anne's reign, and extensively repaired in 1846. The entrance to the chapel was under the central pediment.

PALMER'S ALMSHOUSES in 1817, soon after rebuilding, a drawing by W. Capon.

WHITTINGTON COLLEGE, Archway Road, Islington, is the only considerable group to have been demolished since 1945. They were built about 1822, after an earlier move out of the City, by the Mercers' Company, trustee of the charity, to the designs of their Surveyor, George Smith. The group's destruction by the L.C.C. as part of a road-widening scheme seems to have come about almost by accident. The much-needed road-widening scheme originally threatened only part of the College, vulnerable because as old property it was so much cheaper than more modern commercial buildings which lay in the way of other possible routes. Negotiations with the Mercers' Company revealed that the trustees were anxious to rebuild the almshouses. Despite the fact, therefore, that the group was listed as a historic building (Grade III), and that it formed in the opinion of one commentator 'one of the most attractive examples of early Gothic revival left in London' in the 1960s, no effort was made to save it by either its owners or the L.C.C. as such. The whole property was purchased by the L.C.C., part used for road-widening, and the rest demolished and redeveloped.

## Hospitals

Hospitals, like schools, are particularly susceptible to change, and perhaps need rebuilding even more, as methods of treatment change and improve. Though three at least of London's charitable hospitals were founded in the Middle Ages, most date from the eighteenth and nineteenth centuries, and most have been rebuilt. Many of the demolished buildings were architecturally important as well as being splendid examples of the history of hospital design. It seems a pity that a little more trouble has not been taken to find an acceptable use for outdated buildings, as for example Guy's Hospital has done with its older blocks, or was done with Bethlehem Hospital in Lambeth (now the Imperial War Museum).

A particular loss was ST LUKE'S HOSPITAL, Old Street. The hospital was founded for 'poor insane persons' in 1751 at Windmill Hill and rebuilt to the designs of George Dance, Jnr, in 1782. Like Dance's Newgate Prison, St Luke's Hospital was admired by contemporary critics for being 'characteristic of its uses'. It demonstrates what an impressive building Dance could make even when using humble and unfashionable London stock bricks. The hospital was closed in 1916, and the building became the printing works for the Bank of England. It was demolished in the 1960s.

THE WESTMINSTER HOS-
PITAL was the first to be established by public subscription, in
1720. After two moves, it was rebuilt in Broad Sanctuary in 1834,
to the design of William Inwood
and his son C. F. Inwood. Here
it is about 1870, with the Crimean
monument in the foreground.
The design was welcomed as a
great advance in hospital planning – the wards were grouped
round a hollow crescent. The
hospital was extensively modernised in the 1870s; advantage
was taken of the Gothic design
to add more turrets to the façade
to contain much-needed water-
closets. Despite further alteration
the hospital had become impossibly cramped and insanitary and
in 1936–9 a hospital was built
in the Horseferry Road. The old
hospital was not demolished until
1951, and its site has remained
a car park ever since.

KING'S COLLEGE HOSPITAL was founded in 1839, and
was rebuilt in 1858–60 in Portugal Street, Lincoln's Inn Fields, to
the design of Thomas Bellamy. It was a model hospital of the
period with accommodation for 200 patients. The main block contained the wards, with accommodation for nurses at the rear, and
also at the rear was a lower block containing the theatre.

The impressive staircase was not
only for ostentation but was intended to provide warmth and
ventilation throughout the wards.
The cramped site in the middle of
the densely populated Clare
Market area restricted Bellamy,
but his planning was already
more sophisticated than that of
Inwood. The hospital was moved
to Denmark Hill in July 1913,
and the old building demolished
soon after.

ST THOMAS'S HOSPITAL was originally a mediaeval foundation in Southwark. The hospital was rebuilt in Lambeth in 1868–71, and became the home for the Nurses Training School founded in appreciation of Florence Nightingale's work. Henry Currey's layout of detached blocks with beds for 588 patients at a cost of £332,748 shows the influence of her ideas on the importance of the free circulation of air and the isolation of patients from each other. This plan was adopted from the French hospital at Lariboisère, seen and approved by the officers of the hospital on an extensive foreign tour. The Foundation Stone was laid by Queen Victoria, after some persuasion, on 13 May 1868.

Extensive damage was caused by bombing in December 1940, and since the war Currey's blocks have been gradually demolished to make way for new blocks linked vertically by lifts rather than horizontally by corridors.

## Barracks

For historic reasons, most barracks are sited close to the Royal Parks, which makes their appearance even more important than it would otherwise be. The Government has always had to reconcile the traditional need for a military force in London in the case of civil unrest, with the equally traditional dislike of barracks as neighbours among the middle classes. 'This result is due,' a Victorian civil servant pointed out to Gladstone, 'not so much to the character of the buildings themselves or to their inmates, as to the character of the population which invariably follows any large body of soldiers . . .' On the whole the anti-militaristic tradition in England has meant that barracks have been kept deliberately unobtrusive and as modest as possible, and their quality has depended more on the happy coincidence of an official architect of talent with a period of rebuilding, as with Soane's work at the Royal Hospital, rather than any government's intention to emphasise the importance of the army.

Wellington Barracks, designed in 1834 by Sir F. Smith, with advice from Philip Hardwick, is threatened with rebuilding – its situation rather than any great architectural merit makes its retention desirable.

The only really important barracks to have been demolished in the last hundred years were Knightsbridge Barracks. By 1963 these barracks, however imposing and architecturally fine, were so 'functionally obsolescent' that not even the Victorian Society would fight for them. The accommodation for the men was compared unfavourably with that in H.M. Prisons by Miss Jennie Lee.
Unfortunately, very little effort was made to preserve or re-use the sculpture from Wyatt's flamboyant building, some of which dated from 1795. Most of this, together with other features like the cast-iron gates and railings, found their way into a private scrap-yard. In rebuilding, the Government chose to ignore the advice of the Fine Art Commission which had already warned against the effect of high buildings round the Royal Parks, and added another disastrous tower to those of the Hilton and Royal Lancaster Hotels, thus belittling Hyde Park even further.

KNIGHTSBRIDGE BARRACKS, in 1900, as rebuilt in 1879 to the designs of T. H. Wyatt.

## Prisons

Prisons are not perhaps buildings to be as immediately and obviously regretted as Wren churches or great mansions. However, some London prisons must be numbered amongst her most striking and ingeniously planned buildings.

The nineteenth century saw great changes in the number of London prisons. The famous Southwark prisons – the Marshalsea, the King's Bench, and Horsemonger Lane prisons – were all closed in the early part of Queen Victoria's reign, though the buildings were not demolished till after 1870. The Cold Bath Fields Prison, erected in 1794, and the Clerkenwell House of Correction were both closed in

1877. A number of older prisons were rebuilt in the early nineteenth century like the Tothill Fields Prison, and, of course, all London's present prisons are Victorian, including the doomed Holloway Prison by J. B. Bunning.

NEWGATE PRISON was designed by George Dance the Younger, built 1770–8. Its sombre and grim exterior was said to have been influenced by Piranesi, whom Dance had met in Rome. Contemporaries found it very impressive; Schlesinger, a visitor to London in 1853, described it as 'a gloomy-looking, ancient building. It is the *beau idéal* of prison architecture, with hardly any windows, with here and there an empty niche, or some dilapidated carvings; all besides is gloomy, stony, cold.'

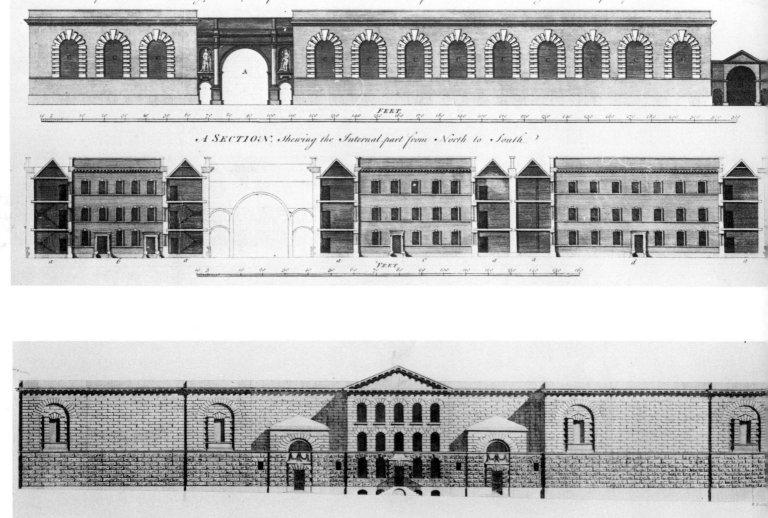

Newgate in 1900. Despite valiant efforts to retain at least the magnificent curtain wall, it was totally demolished in 1902. The condemned cell and other relics were preserved – the condemned cell being built into Lancaster House basement. 'Newgate Prison is to be destroyed,' reported the S.P.A.B. 'Those who have not already heard this will sympathise with us in our disappointment, and it really seems no building of value is safe in London.'

Newgate was next to the Central Criminal Court at the Old Bailey,
later rebuilt on the prison site. There was a certain grim convenience in the arrangement.

THE MILLBANK PENITENTIARY in 1829. Though begun
only ten years after the rebuilding of Newgate, it was a whole
generation away in prison building theory. The plan was that of a
wheel connected at the centre to provide maximum supervision.
This 'panopticon' system, devised by Jeremy Bentham, the philo-
sopher and philanthropist, was later used for other English penal
institutions.
The prison was begun by Thomas Hardwick, and finished by Smirke
in 1816. It was intended to supersede the notoriously unhealthy
'hulks' as a staging post for convicts sentenced to transportation,
but was later used for all convicts and finally as a military prison,
being closed in 1890 and demolished in 1902 for the building of the
Tate Gallery.

# V
# COMMERCE

## Industrial Buildings

Central London has had its share of industry but mostly of the lighter sort. The City was of course full of warehouses for the distributive trades, particularly textiles, but where factories as such were involved they were often for food and drink. It would be difficult to argue for the retention of even light industry in the heart of London, but these industrial buildings were interesting in themselves and had historic links with London's older industries. Some can be, and have been, converted to other uses. Behind their elaborate and often entertaining façades, many of them had extremely up-to-date and architecturally significant structures which pioneered many of the systems on which modern office blocks are constructed. The 1850s and 1860s saw a new generation of City buildings, often partly warehouses with office accommodation as well, towering above their Georgian neighbours, dressed in a variety of styles, but essentially with the façades arranged to reflect the internal arrangement of the building.

DAY AND MARTIN'S BLACKING FACTORY at No. 97
High Holborn, demolished in the 1930s for redevelopment. This
magnificent pilastered frontage with lock-up shops on either side
was built by Charles Day in 1830. The importance of well-blacked
boots is shown by the splendour of the façade, and by the fact that
Charles Day died leaving £360,000. It remained a blacking factory
until 1897, and ended its days as an office building.

Brewing has always been a prosperous London trade, and breweries
and distilleries were among the earliest and finest London factories.
Originally planted in suburban sites, they were gradually engulfed
by houses, and the land became too valuable even for brewing. Of
the most famous London breweries, Reid's famous Griffin Brewery
in Clerkenwell was closed in 1899, Combe's Wood Yard Brewery in
Long Acre in 1905, Meux's enormous Horse Shoe Brewery in the
Tottenham Court Road in 1922 and smaller breweries have been
closed regularly over the last fifty years.

THE LION BREWERY, a prominent riverside landmark in Lambeth, just before it was demolished in 1949 for the building of the Royal Festival Hall. The pilastered building was the storehouse, designed in 1836 by Francis Edwards for the Goding family. As the section shows, the storehouse was massively constructed of load-bearing brick with an all-iron interior, a typical form of construction for Victorian warehouses, with floors of barrel-vaulted brick arches and timber joisting. It became disused in 1924 and badly damaged by fire in 1931, and was almost derelict thereafter. The Shot Tower to the left was retained during the Festival of Britain in 1951 and was afterwards demolished for the building of the Queen Elizabeth Hall.

THE STAG BREWERY site in Victoria, covering some eight acres between Palace Street and Victoria Street, had become an industrial anomaly in the 1930s, but it was not until 1959 that the Bressey road plan of 1937 was implemented. By this a relief road from Grosvenor Place to Victoria Street was driven through the site, and some four office blocks, one over twenty-seven storeys high, piled on the remaining area. This development was significant not so much because of the disappearance of a fine industrial complex, parts of which dated from the early nineteenth century, as because it began the redevelopment of Victoria Street, built in 1850, one of the most important of the Victorian 'metropolitan improvements'.

ROYAL DOULTON POTTERY's showroom and office blocks on the Albert Embankment in 1935, whose demolition in 1952–8 was a loss to the river-side skyline and a unique loss in themselves. Pottery – whether the making of plates or the more prosaic drain-pipe – is one of Lambeth's indigenous industries, carried on in the parish from the seventeenth century, till 1956, when Doulton's shut their pottery and pulled down the last kiln. Henry Doulton amalgamated a number of smaller potteries in the 1860s and 1870s, and was responsible for an important renaissance in the making of English stoneware. He attracted a number of important artists from the adjacent Lambeth School of Art, of whom the most important were probably George Tinworth and Hannah Barlow. These artists made independent figures and plates and vases, and also modelled and painted the terracotta plaques and ornamentation which were such a feature of London buildings between 1880 and 1910, of which perhaps the finest was the Birkbeck Bank (see page 167–9).

Doulton's showrooms were in themselves an advertisement of what the firm could do for any architect who wanted to make use of their products. The smoke from the workshops on the right was led into the 233-foot chimney, whose design, based on that of the Palazzo Vecchio in Florence, is said to have been suggested by Ruskin. The architects were R. Stark Wilkinson, working in close collaboration with Henry Doulton himself. The two large blocks on the Embankment were erected in 1876–7, and demolished together with the chimney in 1952–8.

Fortunately, the smaller block erected at the same time on the corner of Lambeth High Street and Black Prince Road still stands. It was originally used as a museum and library. From its agreeable tympanum showing the making of Doulton pottery by Tinworth, to the High Victorian Gothic detail, it is a monument to a great local industry and an important London material, and should be preserved.

The total destruction of the interior of Soane's Bank of England between 1924 and 1939 is still one of the most unbelievable acts of vandalism committed in London in the twentieth century. A feeling of amazement persists, even after one has read the excellent practical reasons – it was pointed out that the accommodation was inadequate, the external stonework of the lanterns had perished, new foundations were needed, and that saving even one of Soane's halls would have been too inhibiting for the architect and impossibly

The oldest part of the Bank, Sampson's Threadneedle Street façade of 1732–4, with Britannia, the original 'Old Lady' herself. The façade was hidden from the public for much of its existence behind the Front Courtyard, and the later screen wall.

expensive. The Directors' original intention was to preserve some of the interior *in situ* as they did some of the exterior, but Sir Herbert Baker could not resist the greater convenience of re-aligning the building and reconstructing afresh such rooms as Sir Robert Taylor's Court Room, and Soane's halls.

'The Directors', an inspired piece in *The Architects' Journal* explained, in 1925, 'felt that they were less concerned with the abstract architectural values of the buildings of Campbell [*sic*], Taylor and Soane – on some of which the expert critics themselves are not in accord – than with the sentiment to which they give embodiment of the history and association of the Bank.' The claim that they had 'been fortunately able to incorporate in the new design much of the actual Building' is difficult to credit, once one glances at the plans of the old and new Banks, and the only pieces that have survived are some fireplaces, columns and Soane's caryatides, and the statue of Britannia, the Old Lady of Threadneedle Street herself. Whether Baker's marble halls and elaborate pastiches do carry on 'the spirit of the architecture of the Bank' is a subjective decision difficult to make for anyone who did not know the Bank in 1925, but I cannot imagine that this is the case.

Finally, of course, as happens all too often when a case for demolition hangs on the necessity for providing more accommodation on the same site, the Bank *has* had to expand into another site after all.

The rebuilding scheme aroused considerable protest. 'The Bank represents the lifework and masterpiece of one of the most original of British architects,' wrote a correspondent, and went on to warn, only too correctly: 'The persistent destruction of historic buildings in London must in the end reduce the whole to the level of a modern city devoid of that character which lives in the heart of its citizens. By the lapse of time and the universal recognition of its artistic and architectural importance in the history of the nation, the Bank has acquired the character of a historic building which would be included in any true schedule of buildings of national importance.'

The Rotunda, originally designed by Taylor and re-cased by Soane in 1795, under demolition.

The Dividend Office, built by Sir John Soane in 1818–23. This photograph of it taken in 1920 shows the elegant strength of Soane's domes constructed out of hollow pots both for lightness and for protection against fire.

The ingenious Front Courtyard passage turned one of the many awkward corners in the old Bank with skill. Left, a detail of the ceiling.

Soane's work at the Bank is chiefly memorable for his circular top-lit halls, but he also designed the magnificent Old £5 Note Office (1804–5).

One of the pillared screens to the Lothbury Courtyard (1798–9), the main feature of Soane's lay-out. The steps and Corinthian screen with his famous Tivoli capitals was repeated on the other side.

The Garden Court on Good Friday, 1933, with the famous lime tree, some 125 years old, already ringed to kill it. This Court was the graveyard of the church of St Christopher-le-Stocks, absorbed into the Bank in 1781. On the north side was Taylor's Court Room (1766–83) with its fine Venetian windows, left untouched by Soane, but rebuilt by Baker elsewhere.

LOTHBURY in 1843, showing two early banking houses, both of which were demolished during the 1920s. On the right, C. R. Cockerell's London and Westminster Bank of 1837–8. Its restrained trabeated and pillared façade was originally only seven bays wide but was considerably extended. Behind was a fine banking hall nearly 60 feet high. In the foreground is Jones Loyd & Co.'s Bank of 1843 – one of the characteristic banking houses of another banker's architect, P. C. Hardwick, who succeeded Cockerell as Surveyor to the Bank of England. The Renaissance palazzo made a convenient model for an early Victorian bank – it reminded the banker that, after all, he followed in the steps of the Medicis, while it enabled his architect to arrange the exterior of the building to show clearly the object for which it is built'. The very success of these prolific architects has not left them with any memorials – all but one of Hardwick's four banks in the City have gone, while Cockerell's Sun Assurance Office (1839–42) in Threadneedle Street, the last of his City buildings to survive, was demolished for the new Stock Exchange.

THE BIRKBECK BANK at the top of Chancery Lane does not belong to the main stream of bank architecture – it was a splendid rogue elephant of a bank, designed by T. E. Knightley (1823–1905), architect of the Queen's Hall, some ten years before it was opened in 1902. Behind a relatively modest frontage to High Holborn, Knightley created a great banking hall considerably larger than the Rotunda of Soane's Bank of England, some 72 feet across and the whole height of the building. The interior was carried out in Doulton's Carrara ware, relieved by glazed tiles and sixteen murals portraying various aspects of mercantile life drawn from mythology, literature and contemporary life. The broad gallery originally designed for the transaction of associated Building Society business was supported by white gryphons. Though the bank undoubtedly possessed 'une grande allure' in the words of a French critic of 1889, there was also a practical side to the glazed ceramic finish. An architect who visited the bank in 1948 wrote: 'The whole chamber glitters with a glory of freshly washed glazed tiling in a colour scheme of cream buff and brown, with a sparing use of sage green on the lower pilasters and golden mosaic in the dome. Arabesques, diaper patterns and fantastic dragon brackets alike look as fresh as they must have done on the day they were made. . . .'

The dome was framed in cast-iron ribs from which the terracotta panels were hung.

It was a sad example of the ease with which an unusual building can be missed by the planners, and even by the *aficionados*. When the Victorian Society discovered in January 1964 that it was threatened, planning permission had already been given, and the compensation payable had it been withdrawn would have been enormous. The Society reported 'that a direct appeal to the Westminster Bank, with whom the Birkbeck had amalgamated in 1911, proved of no avail, and the bank – inside and out one of the supreme examples of Victorian terracotta decoration – closed for ever in January 1965.'

# Office Buildings

It may seem particularly absurd to argue for the retention of out-dated office blocks. This kind of accommodation is essentially utilitarian, was hardly intended as great architecture, and must be replaced by modern buildings as up to date as the originals were, if commerce in London is to continue to thrive. Broadly speaking these arguments are sound, though they are often used to defend the premature demolition of a sound building to enable some developer to pile a great deal more office space on to the same site. However, against them one must balance the general arguments for keeping variety of buildings even in a commercial area, and for providing an agreeable environment for office workers at lunch-time and in the mornings and evenings, when areas like the City are primarily pedestrian.

It is often possible to retain an interesting piece of street architecture as a façade behind which the accommodation can be re-organised, as was done at the Hop Exchange in Southwark, and in our own day to an 1892 building by Aston Webb and Ingress Bell at Nos 13–15 Moorgate. It can be done with a reasonable profit to the developer or the company redeveloping its own site, but of course is not acceptable to the entrepreneur seeking what is pictur-esquely described as 'maximum profit'.

The following selection of buildings comes chiefly from the City, where a number of equally interesting buildings still linger, but it should be emphasised that the post-war development pattern in the City appears to offer little hope of their survival.

*THE TIMES* ADVERTISING OFFICES built in 1868–74, standing between the vulgar commercial hurly-burly of Queen Victoria Street and the mandarins of Printing House Square. Not in fact the first efforts of the house-breakers, but the effects of a German high-explosive bomb in September 1940. This was re-paired, but the building was demolished in 1962.

The Private House in PRINTING HOUSE SQUARE, originally that of the Walter family, who founded *The Times* newspaper in 1785, and retained a proprietorial interest until 1966. The house, perhaps of greater historic than architectural interest, dated from the eighteenth century, and remained a dwellinghouse until 1910, not only one of the last in the heart of the City, but also the last in which a newspaper proprietor lived 'over the shop' in this way. The editorial offices on the right-hand side also dated from the eighteenth century, though the third floor was added in 1830. The plaque over the door commemorated *The Times*'s crusading days and the City's gratitude for the newspaper's exposure of a commercial fraud in 1841.

The Private House and its garden behind together with the whole of Printing House Square was demolished when *The Times*'s offices were rebuilt in 1962.

The WESTMINSTER INSURANCE OFFICE, at No. 429 The Strand, on the corner of Agar Street, designed by C. R. Cockerell in 1831–2, and pulled down in about 1906 for the British Medical Association building, now Rhodesia House. Though we can see that the future lay with the general-purpose office block, many of the most memorable nineteenth-century buildings were provided for individual clients. Insurance companies were ahead even of joint stock banks in realising the value of a prominent building in attracting public confidence and business.

No. 112 The Strand, perhaps Sir Charles Barry's smallest commission, built for the Art Union of London. This was a splendid middle-class co-operative for those interested in art, founded by Henry Thomas Hope and others. It was run on the lottery system, tickets being drawn annually for artistic prizes which ranged from Parian-ware statues to engravings of contemporary masterpieces. The building survived the Art Union, ending its days as a hosier's shop and being pulled down in the 1930s.

MUDIE'S LIBRARY, at No. 30 New Oxford Street, another centre of middle-class culture, founded in 1844 and finally put out of business by the public libraries just before the Second World War. This building was opened in 1860 and was abandoned by Mudie's in 1930. It was damaged in 1943 and has been a derelict building site since the war, presumably waiting for the new British Museum Library to be built. The scale of Mudie's Library, which had several branches, is shown by the fact that they took 2500 copies of the last two volumes of Macaulay's *History of England* for circulation.

PEAR'S SOAP OFFICE, at Nos 71–5 New Oxford Street, a
'prestige office' of 1887, designed by W. B. Catherwood, with an
Italianate façade in Portland stone and red brick highlighted by
pink and grey Aberdeen granite. Throughout the building's public
areas there was an appropriate emphasis on the virtues of clean-
liness.

The entrance hall was designed to resemble the atrium of a Roman
house, with decoration in mosaic and painted panels in the Pompeian manner. It was adorned with marble statues, and a staircase
in the rare Fiore di Pesca marble led upstairs to the counting-house,
briskly contemporary in style, and a gallery fitted up to exhibit
the firm's collections of works of art.

Most of these had business connections – the firm's paintings
included not only the well-known 'Bubbles' by Millais (for which
they paid £2200 and £20,000 for the first edition of coloured prints)
but also 'This is the way we wash our Clothes' by Hazlaar, 'The
Bath' by Maynard Brown, 'Man Shaving' by Bellei, and 'Monkey
washing Cat' and 'Monkey shaving Dog' by Trood. These offices
were taken over by the Midland Bank in the 1920s.

NEW BANK BUILDINGS, Princes Street, designed by John Soane for the Bank of England as an office block for letting to prominent City tenants. Though Soane himself described the five 'mercantile residences' as 'presenting more of the appearance of one grand hotel than of several distinct mansions', this vertically divided office block of 1807 still resembled a domestic terrace. It was demolished and rebuilt in 1891.

ROYAL EXCHANGE BUILDINGS of 1842–4, by Edward I'Anson & Son (1775–1853, 1812–88), one of the first commercial buildings, divided horizontally, to be built in London for letting as offices, with arcaded shops on the ground floor.

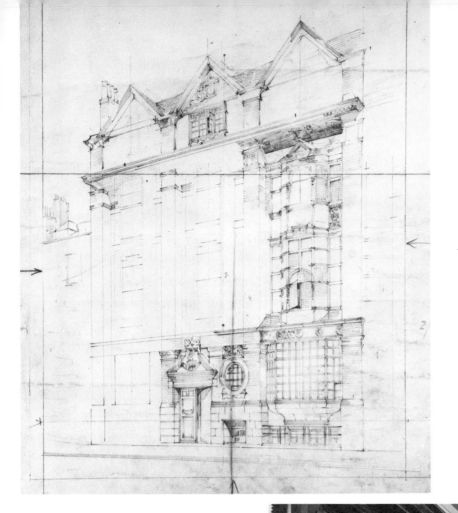

Norman Shaw's NEW ZEALAND CHAMBERS of 1873, at No. 34 Leadenhall Street, a revulsion against the pomposity and foreign magnificence of I'Anson's office blocks. The I'Anson tradition continued in the hands of such architects as John Belcher, whose Mappin and Webb building opposite the Mansion House is now threatened with demolition, and the single sites for which the domestic treatment is most suitable are disappearing. New Zealand Chambers was destroyed in 1940, leaving only Shaw's threatened Baring's Bank to represent him in the City.

The Gerrard Street TELEPHONE EXCHANGE, built for the National Telephone Company in 1907 on the corner of Lisle Street, one of London's first purpose-built exchanges, in which the architect, Leonard Stokes, demonstrated his ideas 'for the logical architectural treatment of a steel-framed commercial structure'. The Elizabethan style of the frontage is extremely restrained and even the name of the building is used as economical and entertaining ornament. The Exchange was taken over by the Post Office and demolished in 1935 to make room for a larger successor.

London's earliest formal commercial building was the Royal Exchange, in which the Stock Exchange actually started business. Throughout the seventeenth and eighteenth centuries the different groups of merchants had their headquarters in various coffee houses, the most famous of which was Lloyd's. Though coffee became an increasingly minor part of the business, the coffee-house system survived well into the nineteenth century, in the Baltic and Jerusalem coffee houses, which only amalgamated to form the Baltic and Shipping Exchange in 1900.

THE BALTIC EXCHANGE passed its last independent years in South Sea House, at No. 37 Threadneedle Street, possibly the City's first prestige headquarters for a joint-stock company. It was built in 1724–5 for the notorious South Sea Company, probably to the design of a little-known architect called James Gould. The Baltic Exchange took it over in 1857, when they moved from the Baltic Coffee House. It had a fine hall on the first floor, originally the Transfer Office. This historic building, here seen in an eighteenth-century print, was demolished for the building of the new British Linen Bank in 1902.

THE JERUSALEM COFFEE HOUSE in Cowper's Court, off Cornhill, was, despite its name, the exchange for merchants dealing with India, China and the Far East, and later on, with Australia. By 1879, the 300 to 400 subscribers had outgrown the old coffee house which dated from the eighteenth century, and Bassett Keeling was employed to design a new exchange, still, however, domestic in scale and still called a coffee house. In 1892, the Jerusalem Exchange moved to Billiter Street, and the coffee house became an office.

Most of the London commodity and other exchanges date from Victorian times, even the older ones like the Corn Exchange being rebuilt. A number were damaged in the war, including I'Anson's Old Corn Exchange of 1881, in Mark Lane, and others like the Wool Exchange of 1875, in Basinghall Street, have been demolished and replaced by an office block.

The new STOCK EXCHANGE seen through the ruins of the old. Not in itself a very important building but one whose demolition and replacement by a twenty-six floor skyscraper is characteristic of the modern City of London. The Stock Exchange moved to its present site in 1801, was rebuilt in 1853 to the design of Thomas Allason, and enlarged in 1885 by J. J. Cole. Cole's end of the Exchange was demolished first in 1967 for rebuilding. Allason's dome, seen here, followed in 1969.

COMMERCE   177

## Coal Exchange

The most famous of the Victorian exchanges was, of course, the Coal Exchange by J. B. Bunning of 1846–9 in Lower Thames Street, and its destruction is one of the great conservationist horror stories, comparable with those of the Adelphi and the Euston Arch. Professor Russell Hitchcock acclaimed it as 'the prime City monument of the early Victorian period' and the 'real London rival' of Labrouste's Reading Room at the Bibliothèque Nationale in Paris.

It was opened by the Prince Consort on 30 October 1849, a historic occasion in itself as it was one of the last on which the river was used for a royal procession.

The cast-iron rotunda surrounded by offices reached from the galleries. A cable motif was used both to ornament the stanchions and for the balustrading, derived from the mine cables and the shipping ropes. Other motifs derived from coal-mining itself were used for the lavish decoration of the building, somewhat damaged after a hundred years but substantially intact. Frederick Sang, one of the foremost decorative artists of the day, was employed to paint the encaustic panels. As well as improbably picturesque views of collieries and colliers, and some jolly miners and miners' tools used to form trophies, there were the more scientific leaves and trees which were fossilized into coal, all forming in Professor Hitchcock's phrase 'a coherent iconographic treatment which is one of the most interesting features of the interior'.

The four-year struggle to save it is extremely depressing, largely because of the City of London's inability to appreciate its own heritage, and also because of the lack of imagination in official town-planning circles in England, which was apparently such that no scheme could be worked out to reconcile the preservation of two important historic buildings with the needs of modern traffic. The problem was that the Coal Exchange and the Custom House of 1813–17 by David Laing faced each other some 49 feet apart across Lower Thames Street, along which an approved through route some 50 feet wide from Blackfriars to the East End, to be finished in 1972, was to run. When the City authorities were told in 1958 that the Coal Exchange was to be listed they told the Ministry of Housing that they proposed to demolish it for road-widening. The Victorian Society joined battle, managing to get the demolition postponed until 1960, and then finding not one but three experts to produce schemes to save it. The Minister delivered judgement on these schemes in January 1962, allowing that Lord Mottistone's scheme, which suggested placing the footways under arcades in the Custom House and Coal Exchange for a short stretch at a cost of £125,000, was 'not impracticable'. None the less he rejected it on the grounds that 'it would involve drastic alteration to the exterior of the building and would substantially reduce the accommodation it provided', thus making it difficult to find a suitable use for it: half a loaf in this case was worse than no bread, even if the half included the magnificent rotunda which most experts considered the finest feature of the building. At a meeting of Common Council on 8 March 1962, following on the Minister's decision, the necessary two-thirds majority for demolition was obtained. Despite an impassioned plea by a former Lord Mayor for saving the Coal Exchange, the meeting appears to have been more in sympathy with Mr D. G. Mills, the Chairman of the Streets Committee, who described it as a dingy place devoid of any paintings or other objects of artistic beauty. As for the much-vaunted ironwork, his widely reported speech continued, he had seen better in boarding houses in Ramsgate and Hastings, and it would not be acceptable for use as public lavatory railings.

In the course of 1962, the Victorian Society pursued a scheme for having the rotunda re-erected, and found a home for it in Melbourne, where the National Gallery of Victoria expressed an interest. On 20 September the City gave the Victorian Society four weeks to find £20,000, half the cost of shipping the rotunda to Melbourne: if this was forthcoming the City would contribute the other half and the rotunda would be saved. This suggestion could not be properly explored as the City insisted on demolition being carried out in November 1962. Now, almost a decade later, most of the site remains a carpark, raising the question of whether the Rotunda could not, by less hasty demolition, have been preserved for re-erection.

## Markets

The market is a very ancient form of trading place, both for wholesale and retail business, but far from abandoned. Recently, both the Portobello Road street markets and the various antique supermarkets in Kensington and Chelsea have shown how attractive to shoppers a number of small retail units grouped together can be: the specialist arcade or market is perhaps the obvious example of the curious and apparent contradiction that similar traders flourish best in a group.

Street markets are, of course, the oldest form, from which evolved both the wholesale markets like Covent Garden Vegetable and Billingsgate Fish Markets, and the neighbourhood market as provided by most pre-1800 developers. In Nash's words, '. . . an open market seems *indispensable* . . . open shambles are essential to the poor and the poorer description of tradesmen who cannot pay large rents . . .'

THE OXFORD MARKET house in 1880, north of Oxford Street on the west side of Great Titchfield Street. It was built about 1724 and opened in 1732 to serve the Cavendish Harley Estate, sited as was usual on the cheaper fringe of the estate. It was demolished soon after this photograph was taken, and a block of flats erected.

In 1869, a Guildhall committee reported that a number of markets had failed and certainly several both in the West End and in poorer areas disappeared between then and 1900. Thus Clare Market disappeared for the building of the Strand Law Courts, in the 1870s, and Newport Market, for that of Shaftesbury Avenue, in the 1880s. The Grosvenor Market at the top of South Molton Street was demolished for the extension of Davies Street to Oxford Street, about 1890; the Portman Market in Church Street, St Marylebone, became a garage.

RANDALL'S MARKET, Poplar, when derelict in 1930. It was founded by Onisiphodros Randall in about 1850.

Probably the most spectacular market architecturally, and certainly the most spectacular failure financially, was the COLUMBIA MARKET, in Bethnal Green, founded for philanthropic rather than commercial reasons by the Baroness Burdett-Coutts in 1864. The Baroness had already built four blocks of model dwellings in the area, and when she heard that the Corporation were planning to extend Billingsgate Market, she decided to found an open market for fish and other provisions which would benefit the East Enders, who were being excluded from the traditional markets, and were ill-served by small local monopolists and the existing unhygienic street markets. An enabling Act of Parliament was obtained and her architect, Henry Darbishire, was commissioned to build a 2-acre market which would elevate the mind as well as serve the more material needs of the neighbourhood. It cost over £200,000, and was opened ceremonially on 28 April 1869. It was in the form of an open quadrangle surrounded by market buildings, of which the galleried market hall was one. There were permanent shops in the surrounding arcades. In the Hall itself, traders of the second class were to occupy twenty-four shops in the aisles, the galleries were set aside for stalls for fruit, roots and flowers, the ground floor was the butchers' shambles, while the centre was reserved for small or fourth-class traders. Though no tolls were charged, the whole elaborate and well-organised scheme was frustrated by the opposition of dealers established elsewhere, afraid for their trade, who prevented wholesalers from supplying the market. The Baroness, who does not seem to have received much help from the City authorities in her attempt to defeat the well-established monopolists, threw her hand in after six months, and handed the market over to the City to run as a rival to its own Billingsgate. This was abortive for the same reasons, and the market was given back to the Baroness in 1874, and finally closed in 1885. The splendid complex was bought by the L.C.C. in 1915, and demolished between 1958 and 1966 for the building of flats, a sterile and unimaginative use for what Professor Pevsner has called 'easily the most spectacular piece of design in Bethnal Green, and one of the great follies of the Victorian Age'.

*Above:* Detail of lamp bracket.
*Left:* The Hall.

Columbia Market in 1915.

The great wholesale markets created and run by the City authorities in Victorian times have been severely affected by modern trading practices. Covent Gardent Market is to be moved, Billingsgate Market may be in danger. The two great meat markets established in Victorian times were the live meat market in the Caledonian Road, which replaced the dangerous and insanitary Smithfield Market, and the London Central Markets erected at Smithfield in its stead for the sale of dead meat and poultry.

THE CALEDONIAN MARKET in Islington, of which the City Architect, J. B. Bunning, complained he had 'prepared an amazing number of plans', was finally opened by the Prince Consort in 1855. Most of the area was naturally taken up with stalls for the animals— some 7000 cattle and 35,000 sheep, 1500 calves and 900 pigs. The central block included a tower not unlike that of an airport controller, from which the manager could survey his domain, a telegraph office and twelve banks. There were two taverns for the graziers and butchers, and four taverns, the Lion, the Lamb, the Black Bull and the White Horse, for the drovers and cattlemen. In the background can be seen the same architect's City Prison, now Holloway Prison.

Though the market became more general and was used both for animals and general merchandise till 1939, in 1965, it was redeveloped and used for housing. The taverns and central tower alone remained.

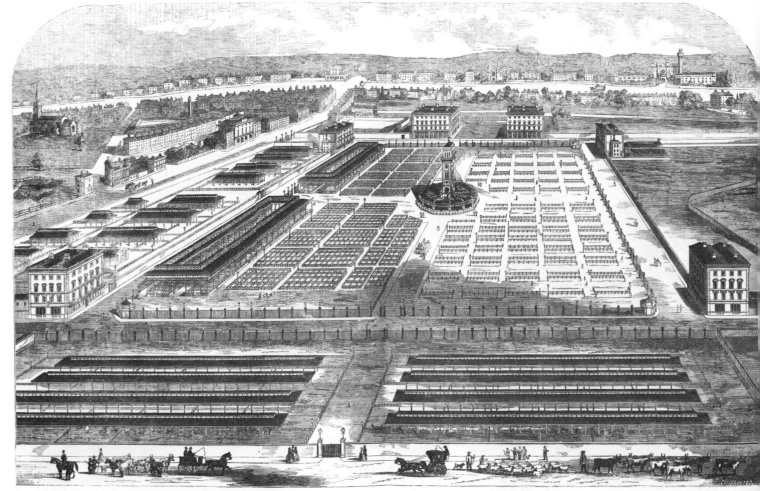

The bazaar or arcade was a very popular nineteenth-century way of grouping small retail shops. Any large space could be converted to a bazaar, as indeed was the interior of the Pantheon theatre, before it became an office. An arcade had to be planned rather than converted, but it was an agreeable and ingenious use for a long narrow site.

A number of West End arcades have survived, though considerably expanded, possibly because of the fuss caused in 1902 by the demolition of the LOWTHER ARCADE for Macvicar Anderson's new Coutts' Bank. The Lowther Arcade was designed by Witherden Young as part of the fine turreted block built in the West Strand in 1831–2, by William Herbert (c. 1792–1863). It was a mere 20 feet wide and 245 feet long, and was the particular province of toy shops. Macvicar Anderson was sufficiently impressed to make a measured drawing of the building in whose destruction he was assisting, an example which more modern architects might copy – though some large commercial offices might find themselves doing a great deal of measuring of historic buildings.

Unlike motor cars, horses and carriages could not easily be sold at the kerbside, and some extremely fine auction rooms were built for their sale. The most famous was, of course, Tattersall's, moved from Hyde Park Corner to Knightsbridge Green in 1865, where horses were sold up until 1939. After the war the valuable 2-acre site was sold, and demolished in 1955 for the building of an office block. It contained stabling and a subscription room as well as auction rooms.

TATTERSALL'S saleroom in 1904. By this time not only was it respectable for ladies to attend sales, Tattersall's was open on Sunday afternoon for the examination of the items to be sold the following day. The gallery was used for carriages as well as spectators.

The classical entrance block on to Knightsbridge Green in 1902, one of the relics which the firm took with it to its enlarged premises in Newmarket.

ALDRIDGES on the west side of St Martin's Lane had been established under another name as a centre for horse and cattle dealing at the beginning of the eighteenth century. The frontage was set back in 1843 when St Martin's Lane was widened, and this new front was designed the following year by the surveyor Charles Hatchard. The firm moved with the times and began selling motor cars in 1907, though it continued to sell horses also until 1926. In 1940 the firm moved to St Pancras, and the building was pulled down in 1955 for the building of Thorn House.

The interior of the building looking towards the entrance in 1844, showing the elegant and practical cast-iron structure which survived until 1955, probably also designed by Hatchard when the front was revamped.

THE PANTECHNICON in Motcomb Street, whose very name was invented by its enterprising creator Seth Smith, provided storage not only for carriages but for wine and other household goods. It also boasted a double row of shops in the neighbouring arcade. It was probably designed by Joseph Jopling, who advised Seth Smith on other occasions, and opened in June 1831. The building retained many of its original features until 1966 when the 'Pantechnicon' organisation moved to cheaper and less central premises and an application was made to redevelop the whole site which stretched from Motcomb Street northwards for three acres. Though the G.L.C. managed to preserve the frontage after serving a Building Preservation Order in June 1965, the historic interior has been lost. Doubtless this was made inevitable by the passage of time, but these features were in their way more remarkable than the façade and deserve recording.

The general office, probably once a reading room for depositors, which retained its original glass partitions and patent iron grate, without an obvious chimney.

The entrance to the vaults where the carriages were originally stored.

The lock-ups with iron doors where nineteenth-century families stored their valuables at the end of the London season. The floors and doors of some of the private storage rooms were similarly covered with cast-iron plates.

## Department Stores

The department store was essentially a French invention, eagerly copied in London and other European capitals in the 1870s and 1880s. The great age of the department stores was 1875 to 1914. Since the First World War the competition of the well-organised multiples has caused the amalgamation, or in some cases the total disappearance, of many famous names, such as Shoolbred's of the Tottenham Court Road, and Glave's of Oxford Street, and since 1960, Gorringes of Victoria, and Woollands of Knightsbridge.

One of the earliest purpose-built stores was MARSHALL AND SNELGROVE of Oxford Street, built in 1876 to the design of Octavius Hansard (1826–97). It was rebuilt in 1968–71.

More typical was the case of SWAN AND EDGAR, of Piccadilly Circus, shown here in 1912, which started in a terrace house in 1812, taking over others in due course. It was rebuilt in 1924–5, as part of the reconstruction which destroyed Nash's Regent Street and the two Circuses.

Shop-fronts are necessarily as subject to changes in fashion as the goods they display. Once they suffer a change of use or cease to catch the eye they are failing to serve their purpose, though like clothes, street frontages seem to return to favour about thirty years later. A whole book could be filled with examples of lost street architecture, and the perceptive London tourist can still spot shop-fronts of many styles, many in danger 'of modernisation'.

Though there are still small shops which claim to be Georgian, Lambert's silversmith's shop, Nos 10, 11, 12 Coventry Street, established in 1803, was probably the largest Georgian shop-front to survive into the twentieth century. It was demolished together with the rest of the north side of Coventry Street soon after 1914, when this photograph was taken by a mourning antiquarian.

COMMERCE 193

# VI
## HOTELS AND
## RESTAURANTS

Coaching Inns

Coaching inns have been so well covered in books on bygone London, that I hesitate to add more about them. However, they were a rare survival of a mediaeval building form into a London of terrace houses, and also a large and important class of specialised buildings which, with one or two truncated exceptions, has been totally swept away. They belonged essentially to the world of the horse-traveller, and once long-distance travel by horse had disappeared they lingered longest as depots and stabling for the carriers and railway companies, rather than as residential hotels or even City pubs. Behind a conventional street façade, they had one or two galleried yards leading through to the stables. Some of the woodwork on the screened galleries is reminiscent of similar screens in eastern countries, whence the coaching inn is said by some authorities to be derived.

The Oxford Arms, Warwick Lane, in 1875, one of the most famous London inns, whose very demolition, in 1876, was a landmark. The Inn, rebuilt after the Great Fire on the site of an earlier hostelry, was closed in 1875, and its threatened disappearance triggered off the formation of the Society for Photographing Old London, without whose photographic records even less would remain of the London demolished between 1870 and 1914.

The GREEN DRAGON YARD off Bishopsgate Within, about 1870. Even when the coaching traffic stopped, stables were necessary for the traveller who drove in his own dog-cart. Note the relatively few bells; in some inns there were lines of ten or twelve. Though the inn dated, in name at least, from the seventeenth century, parts had been rebuilt, and efforts made to modernise the galleries with elaborate screens running up to the full height, and with glazed casements.

196

Southwark was the natural terminus for coaches running southward and particularly south-eastward, and boasted a number of large and important inns including the George, part of which still remains, the Talbot or Tabard, demolished in 1875–6, and the King's Head, pulled down in 1885.

The best known of coaching inns was perhaps the White Hart, described by Dickens as the meeting place of Pickwick and Sam Weller. Only part of the building survived rebuilding in 1868, and the older parts were let out as tenements and to a bacon-curer, and were finally pulled down in 1889.

THE QUEEN'S HEAD, High Street, Southwark, in 1880, apparently an Elizabethan building, whose timber frame had been hidden under modern stucco. It was owned for a short time in the seventeenth century by John Harvard, later the founder of Harvard College, Cambridge, Massachusetts. By 1885, part of the galleries had been let out to a hop merchant, but the inn continued in business till 1895, when it closed. The buildings ended their days as a railway depot.

THE OLD BELL INN, High Holborn, in 1885, again from the Society for Photographing Old London. Superficially it was modern, like the equally famous Bull and Mouth in St Martin's-le-Grand. It was not only the last galleried inn to survive north of the river, it also boasted the last regular service – an omnibus, which daily 'whisked a few country people and their parcels to Uxbridge, Amersham and Wendover'. Bunyer was the last landlord of the Bell; the stone shield commemorates the Gregges, who owned the houses from 1680 to 1722. The building probably dated from the early eighteenth century and survived till 1897.

## Hotels

Hotels in London in the last hundred years fall into three categories, the old-fashioned family hotels, the railway hotels which were the first modern hotels as we know them, and the monster luxury hotels which developed from them, catering not only for travellers, but providing restaurants for the late Victorian and Edwardian upper classes, once dining and lunching out had become socially acceptable. All these types have been virtually superseded by the post-war pattern of hotel concentrating on the provision of bedrooms with the minimum of expensive room-service. In the middle of the nineteenth century London was said to be inferior in hotel accommodation to every capital in Europe with the exception of Constantinople, but despite this need a remarkable number of the hotels built in the following fifty years have been converted to other uses.

The present emphasis on the need for tourist hotels in London obscures the interesting fact that London is full of ex-hotels, abandoned because they were in the wrong place or wrongly designed. It might be well for planners dealing with hoteliers ready to supply the estimated shortfall of tourist accommodation to look round to see what happened to the equally essential tourist hotels of yesteryear.

Among the earliest luxury hotels were the Westminster Palace of 1859 by W. and A. Moseley, the first London hotel to have lifts, now an office block, and the Langham of 1865 by John Giles (died 1900), which opened with a reception for 2000 guests who included the Prince of Wales. These were followed by the Grand, Metropole and Victoria, erected after 1872 at Charing Cross on the site of Northumberland House (see p. 20). The Inns of Court Hotel of 1866 and the First Avenue Hotel of 1884 both stood in High Holborn, and disappeared as even lawyers began to prefer staying at West End hotels. Perhaps the first hotel built for American tourists was Richard d'Oyly Carte's Savoy, opened in 1884–9, and extended in 1904, which has outlived both its neighbour, the Cecil, and its direct rival, the Carlton.

The heyday of the Grand Hotel, complete with Palm Court, Winter Garden and luxurious restaurants, was 1880 to 1914. Such comfortable palaces could be in any dress, the Venetian Gothic of the Langham, the relatively sober glazed terracotta of T. E. Collcutt's Savoy, and the riotous Plateresque of the Imperial Hotel were all acceptable, but perhaps the true Grand Hotel dress was French – like the First Avenue, the Cecil, and César Ritz's own hotels, the Carlton and the Ritz itself.

The first decade of the twentieth century saw the rebuilding of much of Bloomsbury as a hotel quarter. The boom in hotel building was ended by the First World War, and the 1920s and 1930s saw the disappearance of more hotels than the rise of new ones. In the 1914–18 War, a number of hotels were taken over as government offices, and were never returned to their original purpose. The extensions of the Strand Palace and the Regent Palace Hotels, and the building of the Cumberland at Marble Arch in 1933, were amongst the new hotels created for the new mass market. The existing hotels were redecorated for their new clientele, not only rather poorer but younger and gayer than the generation attracted and amazed by M. Ritz's flourishing palms.

## Family Hotels

The West End family hotel was usually started by some old family servant in an ordinary terrace house. They have very largely disappeared or been rebuilt out of recognition, though perhaps

Brown's in Dover Street might claim to represent a vanished class. Thomas's in Berkeley Square and Cox's in Jermyn Street disappeared between the wars; Warren's Hotel in Lower Regent Street became the notorious Continentale and was closed down after a police raid in 1906, which embarrassed a number of well-known patrons. The list could be endless: it must include Morley's Hotel in Trafalgar Square, built in 1831, which became South Africa House in 1921, and also Rosa Lewis's Cavendish Hotel, at Nos 81–4 Jermyn Street, unremarkable architecturally, but which preserved a unique atmosphere until her death, and its rebuilding in 1964.

GARLAND'S HOTEL in Suffolk Street, off the Haymarket, established in the 1840s as a family hotel, destroyed by bombs in 1943 and never rebuilt. Before the 1914–18 War it had the reputation of 'a discreet and famous place to stay', much liked by squires and country gentry. It had its American patrons too, who included Henry James and Harriet Beecher Stowe.

CLARIDGE'S in Brook Street, opened in 1808 by M. Mivart, and sold after his death to Mr Claridge. After the latter's death the hotel was sold in 1895 to the Savoy Hotel management, who pulled down the old terrace houses and rebuilt it as a modern hotel. This contemporary watercolour shows the house at the time of the sale.

The famous Royal Suite in which so many important personages stayed. So well established was this tradition for sovereigns visiting London from choice or necessity, that a story exists that when the Pope was rumoured to be seeking refuge in England in the 1840s, Mr Claridge was approached. So many kings and royal dukes were already resident, he said, that it would be difficult to accommodate His Holiness, but then as His Holiness was a bachelor 'he might not need so many rooms'.

THE TAVISTOCK HOTEL at Nos 4–10, Great Piazza, Covent Garden, was the last group of Inigo Jones 'portico houses' to be destroyed. The western group of the Great Piazza was rebuilt in 1877–9, and the Tavistock was demolished in 1928. The great dining-room occupied the whole of the first floor of the arcade, and kept its early proportions though much of the hotel was repaired and redecorated under the lease granted in 1860. It was a 'masculine hotel' and the traditional London home of sea-captains on leave, for whose benefit a wind-vane was installed in the Coffee Room. When the lease expired it was rebuilt as offices, since the demand for hotels in Covent Garden was small. It was the last surviving member of a somewhat disreputable group of hotels and coffee houses which included the Old and New Hummums Hotels, the Piazza, the Covent Garden and Evans' Coffee House, many of which had theatrical connections.

## Railway Hotels

The railway companies were among the first to operate modern hotels run by a joint stock company with a manager, rather than a private hotel owned and operated by the proprietor. Within a year of opening Euston Grove Station, the London and Birmingham had formed a company to operate hotels in London and Birmingham, and this pattern was followed by others. P. C. Hardwick built the Great Western Hotel at Paddington in 1851–3, and this was followed by those at King's Cross in 1854, Victoria in 1860, St Pancras in 1868, and elsewhere. Even at St Marylebone, the last of the London termini, a 700-bedroom hotel was thought necessary in 1899, though it proved to be the most unsuccessful and shortest lived of all. Most of the hotels have become railway or other offices.

THE ADELAIDE AND VICTORIA HOTELS, as designed by Philip Hardwick in 1839, either side of his Euston Screen. The Victoria on the left was opened as a 'Dormitory', serving breakfast only, under the management of a former Steward from the Athenaeum Club, providing bedrooms at 3/6 to 5/- a night, whose visitors could feed at the more conventional Adelaide, later the Euston, opposite. The two hotels were linked by a clumsy block built over the road in 1881, but as a hotel it was more successful than most, remaining in use until it was demolished in 1962.

The Coffee Room of the GREAT WESTERN HOTEL, designed by P. C. Hardwick in 1952, a building with enormous influence on all its successors, generally acknowledged to be the first really modern hotel. It was embellished externally with turrets, reminiscent of the French chateau style, but also owed something to an English Tudor house, Westwood. Internally the decorations were in the more familiar classical style of the same architect's Shareholders' Room at Euston. As a hotel it was immediately successful, making a profit of ten per cent per annum. In the 1930s both the interior decoration of the hotel and its external ornaments were ruthlessly swept away.

## HOTEL CECIL

'Always for the biggest, their first thought is for the Cecil; and so pass into the courtyard any fine morning in the season, . . . and you will not need to search for the man with the American voice, or the girl with the American smartness. They are everywhere . . .' This was written in 1903, before American entrepreneurs began building hotels for their countrymen, of this leviathan even among Edwardian hotels. Its grand courtyard, shown here decked for the historic visit of the French President in July 1903, opened off the Strand, and the Hotel, like its next-door neighbour the Savoy, extended to the Embankment.

The Hotel Cecil was financed by the group of building societies and other groups headed by Jabez Balfour, which before its spectacular crash in 1892 gave London a number of memorable buildings including Whitehall Court and the Hyde Park Hotel. The Cecil was built on a 3¾-acre site bought from Lord Salisbury, and with its 1000 rooms was said to be the largest hotel in the world, with the possible exception of two (in San Francisco and Saratoga), when it was opened in 1896. It closed in February 1930, and was demolished in the record time of sixteen weeks between September and December, for the building of Shell-Mex House.

The staircase, from a series of photographs taken at the opening of the hotel in 1896, showing the Doulton tiles which decorated the main reception rooms, including the first-floor suite of dining-room, billiard and smoking rooms designed in the Indian style.

'The grand and highly fashionable Carlton is one . . . of the most likely places in London for the foreign potentate or the social star . . . in the Palm Court here one may lounge to perfection amongst the best known people of at least two continents . . . . '

THE CARLTON HOTEL was built in 1899 as part of the same block as Her Majesty's Theatre, Haymarket, which replaced the Haymarket Opera House. The group was designed by C. J. Phipps and the hotel completed by the well-known specialist architects, Lewis H. Isaacs and Henry L. Florence. M. César Ritz, whose association with the Savoy Hotel had just terminated because of a serious clash of temperament, took the hotel and employed his own architect, Mewès, to do the interior in the Ritz manner. It was opened in 1899 and, possibly even more than the hotel which bears his name, was the epitome of the 'Ritz style'. The Palm Court was, of course, the 'great feature', the Winter Garden of the 1880s, revamped in Louis XVI style with a profusion of palms and mirrors. It was here in 1902, after weeks of frantic preparation for what promised to be the grandest London season of all time, that Ritz received the news of the postponement of Edward VII's coronation, a shock which precipitated a nervous breakdown from which the great hotelier never recovered. The hotel survived till 1939, with an increasingly staid reputation. During the Second World War it was bombed.

After the war it remained empty for some years, and in 1956 the whole block was acquired by the New Zealand Government with the intention of building on the hotel site immediately, and of subsequently demolishing Her Majesty's Theatre, a threat which so far has not materialised. The hotel was demolished in 1957–8, thus destroying the unity of a block which expressed the ebullient panache of the Edwardian era better than any other group remaining in Central London.

THE IMPERIAL HOTEL, built on the east side of Russell Square between 1905 and 1911, to the design of Charles Fitzroy Doll (1851–1929), was demolished in 1966, partly because of its lack of bathrooms, and partly because, in the words of the G.L.C., 'the whole frame . . . was so structurally unsound that there was no possibility of saving it if a preservation order had been placed on the building.' It may have been a victim, too, of the time-lag in official taste – it is interesting to see that in 1970–1 the owners of the Russell Hotel, a similar but less extravagant terracotta building designed by Doll in 1898, now on the statutory list of historic buildings, are spending £1 million on restoration, rather than demolishing and rebuilding.

The central and southern blocks of the hotel in 1966. Only a colour photograph could give the true flavour of the red brick, the buff terracotta ornament in which the corbels, gargoyles and statues were modelled, the glazed and gilded sunburst on the façade, and the high green copper mansard roof.

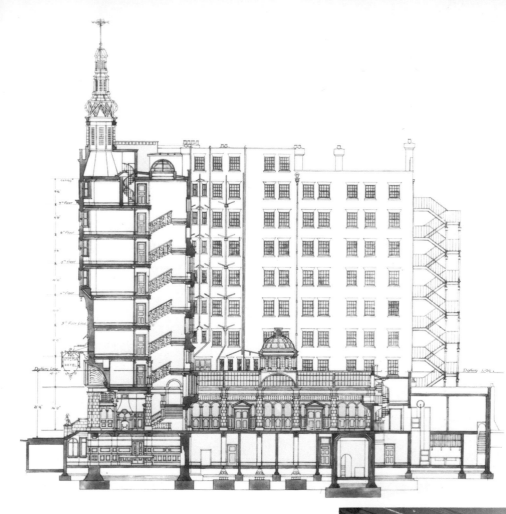

Despite the exuberant Jacobethan façade, given a slightly Spanish flavour by the heraldic ornament, the hotel was ingeniously planned in a straightforward way. This section shows the Winter Garden which occupied the ground floor between the two bedroom wings. The Winter Garden, like the famous Turkish Baths, was decorated in glazed Doulton ware.

The Turkish Baths in 1966.

208

THE BERKELEY HOTEL as rebuilt in 1901, showing how it towered over the neighbouring brick terraces which still lined Piccadilly. By modern standards, however, the hundred-bedroom Berkeley was too small to be economic and a new hotel three times the size is to be built elsewhere.

The Berkeley Hotel site was sold in 1969 for £2½ million, the hotel closed in August 1969 and demolished for office development.

The Berkeley Hotel Buttery was opened in 1933 as a concession to the contemporary need for quick meals. Other parts of the building were redecorated at the same time, but the Buttery itself was perhaps one of the best examples of the 1930s style.

The entrance to the STRAND PALACE HOTEL, 1929, demolished and redesigned in 1968, was one of the last works to survive by an unusual and highly talented architect, O. P. Bernard (1881–1939), responsible for the interior design of many Lyons' restaurants, and hotels in the 1920s and 1930s. Fortunately the dismantled entrance has found its way to South Kensington, where it waits, with many other relics, for resurrection and reassembly.

Bernard's individual use of angular patterns, and the exceedingly successful integration of essential lighting and ventilation into the design of his interiors, made him a most important influence on contemporary designers. The destruction of the Strand Palace entrance seemed surprising at the time, in the light of renewed interest in the 1930s and the use by other fashionable designers at that very moment of the same motifs in echoes of the 1930s style.

Bernard also designed the interior of the Cumberland Hotel, finished in 1933, and its associated Corner House. The writing-room was designed throughout by Bernard, from the characteristic lighting fittings, and engraved glass screens to the furniture and carpets. Understandably the hotel needed redecorating, but unfortunately no attempt was made to keep Bernard's décor intact.

Restaurants are even more subject to the tide of fashion than hotels, dependent like all questions of fashion on the likings and habits of the class and age-group with most money available. Thus eating out was more or less a male prerogative in Queen Victoria's reign, though at the very end it became possible for women to dine in hotel restaurants without causing scandal. In 1918 the cheaper, more light-hearted smaller restaurants began to eclipse the formal ballroom meals of the 'Palm Court hotels'. Café society of a relatively respectable sort emerged, frequenting the famous 'night spots' of the 1920s.

After 1945 the night-club type of restaurant never really recovered its clientele – the 'Upper Three Thousand' who expected to dine out regularly, go to a theatre and on to a night club never re-emerged from the mists of wartime austerity.

Many restaurants are opened in existing buildings, and therefore interior decoration is always more important than external architectural features, often limited to an eye-catching doorway or an up-to-the-minute style of lettering.

The eating room at the LONDON TAVERN in Bishopsgate Street Within, one of the best known of the many banqueting houses in the City and the meeting place of many City clubs. It was rebuilt in 1765–8 to the designs of William Jupp (d. 1788), architect to the Carpenters' Company, but the decoration of the famous Dining-room or 'Pillar room' was carried out by his 'ghost', William Newton (1735–90), whose drawing is shown here. The Tavern was demolished in 1876 for the building of the Royal Bank of Scotland.

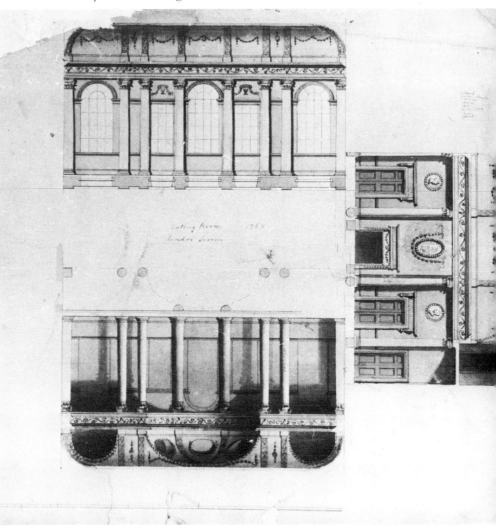

Before its major rebuilding between 1900 and 1930 the Strand boasted not only a large number of theatres but also a number of restaurants. There was Gatti's Adelaide Gallery, at Charing Cross, established about 1860, the Tivoli, pulled down and rebuilt about 1890, but short-lived thereafter, the Gaiety Restaurant next to the Gaiety Theatre, demolished for the making of the Aldwych, and never re-established on its new site.

One of the earliest and best-known was SIMPSON'S, at Nos 101–2 The Strand, opened in 1848 in part of Ries' 'Divan' or public smoking room, where smokers could sit in comfort and play chess if they so desired. The restaurant, on whose arrangement Simpson consulted Alexis Soyer of the Reform Club, specialised in traditional English dishes such as roast beef and lamb chops. Its interior with its hard 'horse-box' benches round the walls was typical of many humbler chop-houses. In 1903–4 the restaurant was bought up and rebuilt as part of the Savoy Hotel. Though the traditional 'bill of fare' – never 'menu' – was retained, the interior was modernised, and other refinements like an Adam décor for the ladies' dining-room crept in.

ROMANO's at No. 399 The Strand in 1885, opened in a re-fronted house by an ex-waiter from the Café Royal. It was typical of many nineteenth-century restaurants with a number of small rooms on several floors. It enjoyed a 'Bohemian' reputation, and was rebuilt on a larger site in 1911, but was closed in 1948.

ST JAMES'S RESTAURANT, at Nos 24–6 Piccadilly, built in 1875 by the owners of St James's Hall, was an architect's restaurant perhaps rather than a waiter's. It was said to be the first restaurant in London to have a small kitchen to each dining-room, 'an indispensable adjunct to hot and rapid service'. The front was designed in Venetian Gothic by Walter Emden, a well-known theatre architect, in sympathy with the front of No. 28 Piccadilly designed in 1855 by Owen Jones. The Restaurant was demolished with the Hall for the building of the Piccadilly Hotel.

213

THE CAFÉ ROYAL at No. 68 Regent Street, a legendary institution created not by its architecture but by the literary and social demi-monde which made the Café its headquarters between 1885 and 1914. It was opened in 1865, and expanded rapidly, ultimately including the Restaurant upstairs, the Grillroom, a masonic suite, and other less reputable private rooms, but *the* historic Café Royal was the Brasserie or Domino Room downstairs, decorated with Italian caryatides between the vast mirrors, and lined with its famous red benches and marble-topped tables. In its hey-day, it was a curious mixture of the artistic and literary world – no restaurant has been painted or written about so many times – and the sporting underworld. Whistler held court here, as did Frank Harris, the influential editor of *The Saturday Review*, but it was Oscar Wilde who entertained the most brilliant circle – which included Max Beerbohm, William Rothenstein, Aubrey Beardsley and, most tragically, 'Bosie', Lord Alfred Douglas. After Wilde's trial the Café suffered a certain eclipse, but became in due course the haunt of other well-known figures. The stream of names is endless, and the Café Royal mystique came to irritate some, so much that one newspaper commented that it had been 'artistic London's hot-air cupboard' for nearly fifty years. Like the rest of Regent Street it was rebuilt in 1924–8, and many of its old patrons scattered to smaller, more old-fashioned restaurants which had kept their Bohemian flavour. Some felt that the fine new Café lacked not only the dominoes but the magic of the old, and demanded with Augustus John, 'What have you done to my Café?' The Brasserie finally disappeared in 1951, when the red plush benches and the marble-topped tables were removed.

THE CAFÉ MONICO was promoted from an obscure site in Tichborne Street by the building of Shaftesbury Avenue in 1888–9. Their new building was a complex of restaurants typical of the period, including the Gallery dining-room (*below*), modelled on the famous Adelaide Gallery at Gatti's, where the Monico brothers had been in partnership. Terracotta was used extensively for ornament both on the Shaftesbury Avenue façade and inside. The building was demolished in the 1950s for the proposed rebuilding of Piccadilly Circus, a project which has hung fire so long that the Café Monico site seems likely to become even better known than the restaurant.

THE HOLBORN RESTAURANT, demolished in 1955, was possibly the largest as well as the last of the huge Edwardian restaurant blocks. In addition to its Grand Restaurant, shown here in 1935 ready for dancing and cabaret in the evening for those well-known people whom the management claimed 'lunch here daily, dine here nightly', it had fourteen other restaurants and private dining-rooms, and three masonic temples. After a chequered early career as first a casino, then a swimming bath and a dance hall, it opened as a restaurant in 1874, being extended and redecorated in 1896, and partially redecorated in the 1930s. Its four-day sale in June 1955 provided not so much a microcosm as a macrocosm of middle-class eating habits in the first half of the twentieth century. Its scale is shown by the fact that over eighty dozen chairs were included.

The Empire Grill Room (*left*) had 1896 terracotta decorations. The Holborn's fate was typical, and shared by such competitors as Fascati's in Oxford Street and most of the Lyons' Corner Houses established between 1910 and 1928 for the mass middle-class market.

Public houses have declined steadily in number over the last century. At first this was due to the ugly image they had acquired as dens of vice in which the honest working man was tempted to part with his earnings on his way home to his wife and family. In the words of a critic in 1880, 'If there are four houses that a man has to pass, he is likely to go into one of them, whereas he may escape if there is only one. . . .'

Both public and private redevelopment schemes therefore envisaged the extinction of some of the existing public houses, which was made easier by the vulnerable corner-sites which so many pubs occupied. This tendency continued between the wars and was adopted by the brewers themselves, though possibly for economic rather than moral reasons. A number of pubs were bombed and never rebuilt, and in the last twenty-five years a system of 'rational-isation' has reduced the number of London pubs, in a manner unhoped for by the keenest Blue Riband campaigner of the 1890s. With amalgamation among breweries and the reduction in the variety of beers sold, there is logic in the closing down of the out-lets – one figure for redevelopments was put at two new pubs for seven old.

The famous EAGLE TAVERN in the City Road, of 'Pop goes the Weasel' fame, bought by the Salvation Army in 1882, and run reluctantly by them as a public house for the statutory six months before the licence could be terminated.

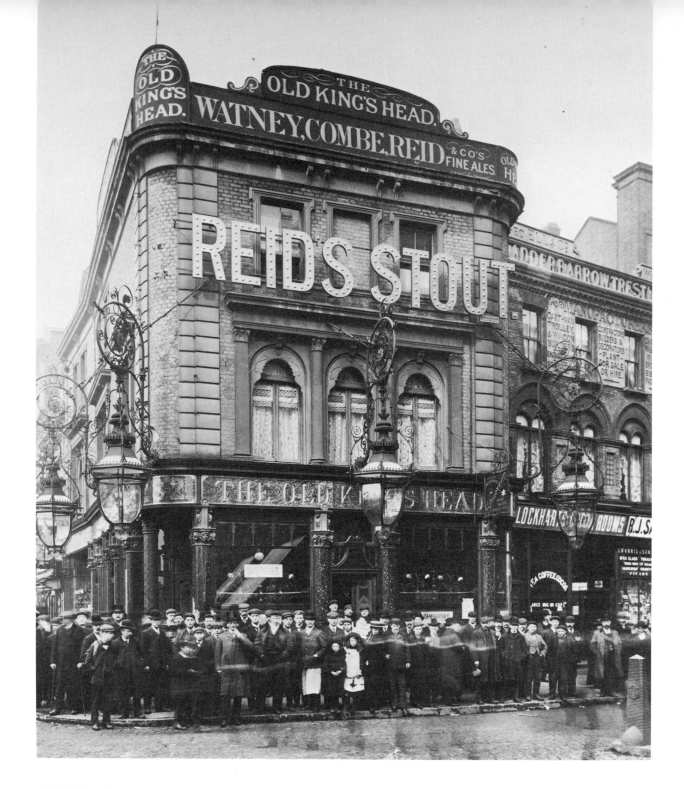

THE OLD KING'S HEAD, a 'gin palace' of about 1880, on the corner of the Euston and Hampstead Roads, demolished for road widening about 1906. It is difficult to imagine the glittering effect of the cut-glass lamps in a gas-lit street, and it is harder to blame slum-dwellers for finding their warmth and cheerfulness attractive.

THE ROYAL SUSSEX ARMS
and the GEORGE, Hammer-
smith Broadway, in July 1910,
also demolished for road-widening but early victims of 'rational-
isation'. Both the early nineteenth-century Royal Sussex and
the much earlier George gave
way to a monstrous new George
decked out in the most sophisticated terracotta decoration, which
still stands.

The two Georges in July 1911.

THE ARCHWAY TAVERN, Highgate, one of the many rural or suburban pubs lavishly rebuilt in the 1880s and 1890s. It was succeeded by a large new hotel in the French style complete with mansard roof, as bang up to the minute as the horse trams which succeeded the horse buses at the same time.

THE STAR AND GARTER, Putney, in 1881, before rebuilding in 1901. The Embankment did much to destroy the charm of London's riverside in its lower reaches, in most cases actually leaving riverside buildings with their own landing places high and dry.

# VII
# TRANSPORT

## River Thames

London's oldest highway is her river. To the quays and piers of the port of London came foreign traders in their ships, coasters from other British ports with indigenous cargoes, and in due course British ships laden with foreign cargoes for native consumption or re-export. Until the nineteenth century the Thames was also a major traffic route for Londoners and, to a lesser extent, an important inland waterway. It was a broad, fairly sluggish stream flowing between marshes and easily flooded fields in its upper reaches, almost non-tidal above old London Bridge, whose narrow arches acted as a weir. With the building of new London Bridge, opened in 1831, the tide came above the bridge regularly, and with the embanking of the Thames, the narrowed stream became faster and more dangerous for small boats.

In Victorian eyes the river had considerable social advantages which we are perhaps unwise to ignore, being 'a highway subject neither to the wear and tear, nor the expensive repairs, nor the dusty and inconvenient transit, in dry weather of ordinary roads; and by which no one can travel without . . . enlarging his stock of health'.

The Victoria and Albert Embankments built in the 1860s destroyed the wharves which lined the Surrey side of Lambeth Reach, and many of those on the Middlesex shore between Westminster and Blackfriars Bridges. A number lingered on Millbank upstream of the Victoria Tower until 1900, and were then cleared away for road improvements.

The penny steamers ran from Woolwich to Chelsea, providing a fifteen-minute service to no less than twenty-seven piers. In 1908 they were withdrawn, and though some piers are still used by mere pleasure steamers, a good many have actually disappeared. This view of a steamer leaving Lambeth Pier, just upstream from St Thomas's Hospital, was taken in 1907.

The improvement of the road surfaces in Central London, as these were taken over first by the Metropolitan Board of Works in 1856, and by the L.C.C. in 1889, removed the need for river transport for people. The railways usurped the place of water transport for heavy cargoes of building materials and coal. In the last ten years the closure of the Docks has meant the end of the barge traffic on the river: very little now goes up or down except some fuel oil and a lot of refuse.

The City's wharves were particularly important, and up until 1939 the northern shore between Blackfriars and Tower Bridges was lined with working warehouses, some of them of great antiquity.

One of the finest was PAUL'S WHARF, standing just below the Cathedral, here shown before 1890, when the eastern block, on the right, was rebuilt. The house in the middle, containing no less than nineteen rooms, was let out in lodgings, and was said to be the last riverside private house. It was reputed to have been occupied by James I, who was said to have lodged his soldiers in the left-hand block, from which it took its name of 'barracks'. The old house and the 'barracks' were demolished in 1898.

A much more recent serious loss is that of QUEENHITHE DOCK, where the buildings were demolished in the spring of 1971 for the building of yet another tourist hotel. This was particularly regrettable since Queenhithe dated from Saxon times, and was probably the oldest dock in the City as well as the last. The dock had an unusual plan in the form of an 'H' – the lower half being dock open to the river, and the upper half a turning square for vehicles giving on to Upper Thames Street. The dock was divided into two wharves – Abbey Wharf belonging to the Fishmongers' Company, and Smith's Wharf, which had belonged to the City Corporation itself since the seventeenth century. This had an extremely fine mid-nineteenth-century warehouse in yellow stock and gault bricks, said by one authority to be the finest warehouse of its kind left in the City.

The surrounding buildings, though not as important individually, made an interesting group, of such importance as to be on the City's original list of conservation areas – a designation keenly supported by the G.L.C. Historic Buildings Board.

However, just before Christmas 1970, a private developer, Mr R. G. Lawrence, acting, according to the City planning office for a group of Norwich businessmen, applied for outline permission for a 300-bedroom hotel at Queenhithe. On the strength of fuller but still conditional approval, granted in February 1971, from the City Corporation, the planning authority, demolition of part of Queenhithe began in the spring of 1971, presumably to secure the magic bonus of £1000 a room for hotels on which work began before 31 March 1971. The total government grant payable on this development, if completed within two years, has been estimated at £300,000. It surely shows a ridiculous failure of planning when a developer is receiving a government grant to destroy buildings which another government department has indicated strongly, if unofficially, that it would like to see preserved.

Though one must accept that such a dock will no longer be used commercially under modern circumstances, the City planners seem to have made no effort to find a new use for such interesting buildings on such an important site. It could perhaps have been retained as a public landing place for pleasure craft. After the proposed Thames barrage is built the river will be a great deal safer for amateur sailors, but it is not now easy to go ashore. Though, of course, a number of 'public stairs' and landing places dating from mediaeval times still exist, they are now being rapidly extinguished as inconvenient nuisances by private owners and public authorities alike.

It is an example of the damage brought about by the inadequacy of the City list drawn up in 1947, when little attention was paid to such fine Victorian buildings. This list is in process of revision, and the City is now designating its conservation areas, so it can be hoped that such losses will not continue.

St Katherine's and the London Docks in 1938 ; the only docks to have buildings of real importance.

One of Philip Hardwick's warehouses at St Katherine's is to be preserved, but those at the London Docks, designed by Daniel Asher Alexander in 1796, are in danger.

'Everything here is on so grand a scale that the largest component part is diminished; the quay, broad enough to build several streets abreast; the square, open stretches of gloomy water; and beyond these the wide river. . . . It is a great plain; a plain of enclosed waters, built in and restrained by the labour of man, and holding upon its surface fleet upon fleet, argosy upon argosy. Masts to the right, masts to the left, masts in front, masts yonder above the warehouses.' Richard Jefferies' marvellous description of 'Venice in the East End' in 1884 has the additional charm of nostalgia today. Four major London docks have been closed in five years: the East India Docks were closed in 1966, St Katherine's followed in 1968, the London Docks in 1969, and the enormous Surrey Commercial complex of some 400 acres in 1970. It would be impossible to ignore the loss of such a large area formerly dedicated to such a fundamental traditional London occupation.

St Katherine's Dock as originally planned in 1836.

Before 1750, Londoners depended on one bridge only and a host of ferries and watermen, partly because travel by water was easier, and partly because of City opposition to any competition for old London Bridge. With the building of Westminster Bridge in 1750 to the design of Labelye, the monopoly was destroyed, and in the century that followed six more bridges were built between Battersea and the City. The last four – Chelsea (1858), Lambeth (1862), Albert (1873) and Tower (1886) Bridges – followed shortly after. By their very nature bridges age more rapidly than other buildings, and in a thriving commercial community it is difficult to defend the retention of an inadequate or a dangerous structure. On the other hand, there seems to be increasing evidence that road-widening and bridge-widening and rebuilding are no better ways of getting rid of traffic than Danegeld was as a way of getting rid of the Dane.

London, unlike many of her continental peers, has long since lost her mediaeval bridge, and during the last 110 years has rebuilt all her other bridges, possibly because their relative scarcity leads to their rapid destruction by heavy traffic. Aesthetically, this has often been a change for the worse, particularly in the loss of the nineteenth-century suspension bridges.

Easily the oldest and most picturesque bridge to disappear in the last hundred years was old Putney Bridge, built entirely of wood in 1726, seen here in 1881 from Putney Church tower looking towards Fulham, whose church is on the left. There was a slightly wider central span, known as Walpole's Lock (after Sir Robert Walpole, who helped to promote the Bridge Bill), to help river traffic to negotiate the narrowly spaced wooden piers. A new bridge was built slightly upstream in 1884–6, and the old bridge demolished soon after.

The old Toll House on the Fulham side of Putney Bridge, with a flat-bottomed Thames sailing barge built with a collapsible mast to enable her to negotiate the bridges.

The bridge was built to replace an ancient ferry, and was supported by tolls. These were abolished in 1880, amid considerable local rejoicing.

WATERLOO BRIDGE was built between 1811 and 1817 to the design of the elder John Rennie (1761–1821), whose equally talented son, Sir John Rennie (1794–1874), also worked on its actual construction. It was described as the finest of the Thames bridges, and the 'most famous English structure of the nineteenth century'. The two-lane bridge was already proving inadequate for modern traffic in 1923, when it was discovered that three of the bridge piers, on their wooden piles, were sinking, one by as much as 28 inches. The dilemma before the London County Council, who were responsible for the bridge, was whether to demolish and rebuild the bridge twice as wide with four lanes of traffic, or to go in for extensive repair, which would be hardly less expensive. They decided to rebuild in 1926, but were persuaded to wait for the report of a Royal Commission, appointed as a consequence of public pressure, whose terms of reference were cross-river traffic from Hammersmith to Woolwich Tunnel. The witnesses included the spokesmen for an extremely distinguished professional group representing the Royal Academy, the R.I.B.A., the Town Planning Institute, and the Society for the Protection of Ancient Buildings, organised to save the bridge, which put forward a number of feasible proposals.

The L.C.C.'s point of view was well put by John M. Gatti, the Chairman of the Finance Committee:

'. . . if . . . the only function of the bridge is to be beautiful, or that if it is beautiful it can dispense with performing other functions, I have nothing more to say; but if you hold that the first function of Art is to add beauty to utility, and that utility must come first, and that a growing city with growing demands must perforce sometimes have to let things go . . .'

The Commission came up with a comprehensive and far-reaching scheme which they thought would solve London traffic problems for three decades. Four piers of Waterloo Bridge would be taken down and rebuilt on new concrete foundations, it would be widened, and new bridges at Charing Cross and Blackfriars, originally suggested in 1854, should be built. The L.C.C. agreed to this scheme on condition that the central government would meet seventy-five per cent of the estimated cost of the Charing Cross Bridge, some £7½ million. However, the money was not in the end forthcoming, and finally the L.C.C. had to foot the bill itself, deciding very practically to spend £1,295,000 on a new four-lane bridge, rather than £1,081,000 on repairing the old. The struggle continued for some years, and reached constitutional proportions: in February 1932, the L.C.C. voted by an overwhelming majority to rebuild Waterloo Bridge; on 1 June the House of Commons threw out a clause referring to the new bridge from the London County Council Money Bill. This was, however, only a postponement, and at a time when the national economy was in a poor way the British Government were not prepared to spend money on art or, equally characteristically, on long-term but expensive solutions to major problems. The L.C.C. were paying the piper, and had to be allowed to call the tune, however philistine. The bridge was closed in June 1934, and demolition started at once. Symbolically, it was Herbert Morrison, then Leader of the L.C.C., who removed the first stone on 20 June.

Its destruction was tragic, epitomising as it did the conflict between the local ratepayer and the national lobby for the preservation of art treasures of more than local importance. The L.C.C. does seem to have been determined to demolish the bridge, but Waterloo Bridge's destruction was largely due to the refusal of the national Government to contribute in a realistic way to the preservation of a national monument. This cheese-paring attitude will continue until sufficient funds are allocated by Parliament, as a matter of course, for the preservation of such monuments.

WATERLOO BRIDGE in 1845. An early photograph by Fox Talbot taken before the making of the Victoria Embankment.

A contemporary engraving showing the construction of the bridge and the wooden piles which caused the sinking.

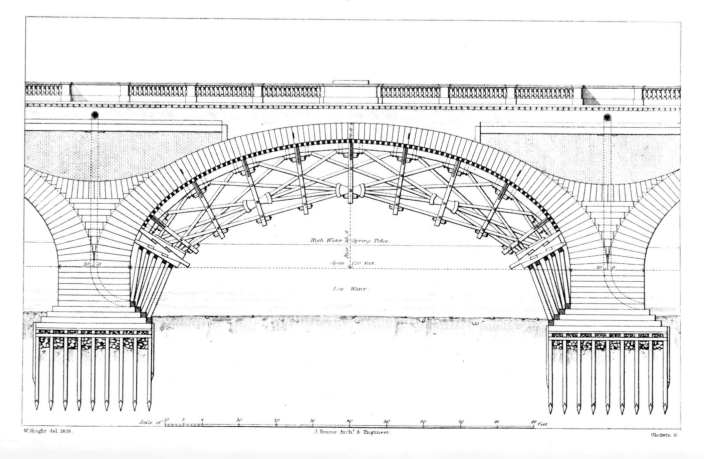

CHELSEA BRIDGE, opened in 1858, like Battersea Park, is one of the achievements of the Commission for Metropolitan Improvements. Its magnificent ironwork was designed by Thomas Page, the engineer of the Thames Embankment from Vauxhall to Chelsea Bridge, though by 1929 when this photograph was taken it had lost some of its ornate spikes. It was rebuilt 1936–7. On the right is the chimney of the Western Pumping Station, a rare survivor of the elaborate factory chimneys built by Victorian engineers.

Suspension bridges were extremely fashionable in the mid-nineteenth century. Even St James's Park had one over the lake (demolished in 1957). Chelsea was followed by Lambeth Bridge in 1862, very narrow and closed to vehicular traffic in 1910, rebuilt in 1932–9, and Albert Bridge.

LAMBETH BRIDGE from Millbank in 1896, looking towards
Lambeth Palace. The new bridge was built upstream of the old. All
these old houses and wharves were swept away in the 1920s and
1930s in the building of I.C.I.'s Thames House and the 1929 rebuilding of Lambeth Bridge.

LONDON BRIDGE about 1905 as designed by Rennie, and opened by William IV in 1831. It was built to replace the mediaeval bridge of Peter de Colechurch, finished in 1209.

Rennie's bridge, widened in 1902–4, was a victim of motor traffic – heavy lorries and other vehicles, of which some 50,000 a day were calculated to cross it, were causing settlement of the pier foundations. Because over 70,000 pedestrians a day also used the bridge, demolition and rebuilding have been carried out while the bridge remains in use. Begun in 1968, it will be finished in 1972.

Many of the buildings in this book are obvious victims of official parsimony or penury; it might be said that London Bridge was to some extent a victim of civic affluence. This is because London Bridge has been endowed by pious Londoners since mediaeval times, and the City Corporation were rich enough to spend £4¼ millions on rebuilding Rennie's bridge, immediately the problem became apparent. The fabric of the bridge was sold to an American development company for re-erection in Arizona for £1 million.

Euston Station

'Its destruction is wanton and unnecessary – connived at by the British Transport Commission, its guardians, and by the London County Council and the Government, who are jointly responsible for safeguarding London's major architectural monuments, of which this is undoubtedly one. In spite of . . . being one of the outstanding architectural creations of the early nineteenth century and the most important – and visually satisfying – monument to the railway age which Britain pioneered, the united efforts of many organisations and individuals failed to save it in the face of official apathy and philistinism. . . .' Thus the *Architectural Review*, the doyen of English architectural journals, began a measured denunciation of the 'long drawn out history of bureaucratic dilatoriness and evasion which led up to the actual demolition . . .' of the Euston Arch, a detailed account which should be read by anyone interested in this incomprehensible story. ('The Euston Murder', *Architectural Review*, April 1962.)

Euston Station was not only the first London terminus, it was the first railway station in the world in any capital city. It was therefore a particularly important monument to the Railway Age, the more so because it was conceived on a heroic scale. It was designed by Philip Hardwick (1792–1870) in 1834–8. The London and Birmingham Railway was opened in September 1838.

The Arch did not remain in splendid isolation (page 203) for long, and in 1846–9 the terminus was enlarged by P. C. Hardwick (1822–1890) in a fine robust Italianate style instead of his father's more remote Doric. The two major features of this were the Great Hall, shown here in Hardwick's Royal Academy drawing and the Shareholders' Meeting Room in the same central block, photographed in 1958.

235

In 1959, when the British Transport Commission came to redevelop the Station, they appear to have ignored the fact that both the Arch itself and the Great Hall (1846–9) were listed Grade II, though an early scheme did suggest the preservation of the Arch by its removal. Their first formal proposal to demolish the Arch was put forward in January 1960, and the L.C.C. as the planning authority accepted that the Great Hall could not reasonably be kept. They suggested that the Arch should be re-erected somewhere suitable nearby. The Commission, however, refused to accept the financial responsibility for this.

In the spring of 1960 the Fine Art Commission, the national watch-dog over such artistic problems, to whom the matter should have been referred but had not been, actually had to ask both parties to consult them. This inconvenient request was successfully evaded by the B.T.C. referring them to the L.C.C. who suggested that the Ministry of Housing and Local Government might be the one to call them in. This the Ministry refused to do since the matter was still officially before the L.C.C.

In May 1960 the Minister was asked to place a Building Preservation Order on the Euston buildings, something he felt to be unnecessary as the L.C.C. was in touch with the B.T.C. over the problem. In June 1960 the Fine Art Commission wrote to the Minister pointing out their concern for the Arch, and again asking to be consulted over the proposals not only for the demolition of the old but also the erection of a new station. This again was ignored – The Minister had not answered the Commission's letter four months later. It was not until July 1961 that the Minister finally revealed – in the most unobtrusive manner possible, a written answer to a parliamentary question – that the Government had decided that they could not afford the £180,000 needed to dismantle and re-erect the Arch. Public disquiet over the situation had continued throughout this period of official inaction, despite a rather naïve feeling that where such an important public body as the B.T.C. and a local authority with such a fine record of concern for architecture and town planning as the L.C.C. were concerned nothing really disgraceful could occur. Further public agitation continued, led by the President of the Royal Academy, backed up by the three major national amenity societies, the S.P.A.B., the Georgian Group and the Victorian Society, and the London Society, culminating fruitlessly in a visit to the Prime Minister (then Mr Harold Macmillan) on 24 October 1961. Both Arch and station were demolished in the course of the following year.

The technical arguments are complex, and there is no space to analyse them fully. However, it must be said that there is no reason to suppose, if the preservation of the Arch and possibly even of the

Great Hall had been made a design requirement of the new station, that it would have been beyond the professional competence of British Railways' architects to incorporate them successfully, as Italian architects managed to do with part of an ancient wall in Rome. This is borne out by the disquieting suggestion, made since the new station has been erected, that even with the longer platforms necessary for modern trains, the Arch could have been left *in situ* without grave inconvenience.

'The Euston Murder' reflects no credit on anyone concerned: the B.T.C., whose architects lacked the imagination to see the advantage of incorporating the old Arch in their new station; the L.C.C., who were unable or unwilling to force the B.T.C. to behave responsibly and submit their plans for a new station before destroying the old; and above all the Government and the Ministers concerned, who lacked either the interest or the authority to prevent the Government-appointed watchdog, the Fine Art Commission, from being snubbed for doing its job. The only person who emerges with credit from the affair is the demolition contractor, Frank Valori, who offered to have the stones of the Arch itself numbered on his own initiative in case of an official change of heart.

The fight to save the Arch was not perhaps as totally useless as it appeared in 1962, for latent public opposition to such acts of destruction was altered and organised as never before, and has been growing since. The public protest which greeted British Rail's proposals to demolish both King's Cross and St Pancras in 1966 was as much a memorial to the Euston Arch as the model of the Arch presented to the Victorian Society by Frank Valori.

The Great Hall under demolition in July 1963.

# THREATENED BUILDINGS

The threats to historic buildings are very much smaller today, in many important respects, than they have been during the period covered by this book. They are better protected by legislation, and public opinion is more aware of the need to protect them and to make sure that such protection is carried out than ever before. At the same time, unfortunately, there are valid social and economic reasons why a historic building *may* have to go because of the needs of roads or hospitals or even normal commercial redevelopment which could be rendered impossible by the retention of a building in a key site. There are also whole classes of structure, such as the warehouses which line the Thames from the City eastwards, and outer suburban churches, which are becoming redundant, and which will either have to be converted, or demolished and the site redeveloped.

Some of the buildings now threatened can be saved, others may have to go if the cost of preserving them is too great, either in terms of money or of inconvenience in planning terms. Public opinion can at least make sure that the alternatives to demolition are properly explored.

*Opposite*
1. Rule's Restaurant, Covent Garden.
2. 448–9 The Strand.
3. Holy Trinity, Bishop's Bridge Road.
4. Highgate Cemetery.
5. New Scotland Yard.
6. Albert Bridge.

*Below*
St Pancras (*left*) and King's Cross Stations.

1

2

3

4

5

6

# List of Illustrations

The author and publishers are most grateful to all those who have lent photographs for this book. In those few cases where we have been unable to ascertain the copyright position before going to press we would like to hear from the copyright holder in order that we may give them due acknowledgement in later impressions. For the sake of brevity the main sources of illustrations are designated with the following abbreviations.

B of E    The Governor and Company of the Bank of England
CL        Country Life
G         Guildhall (Corporation of London)
GLC       Greater London Council Photograph Library and Print Collection
GO        Grosvenor Office
NMR       National Monuments Record (Crown copyright). Prefix BL indicates a photograph by Bedford Lemere
Olney     From the collection of the late E. P. Olney reproduced by courtesy of Peter Gerhold
RIBA      Royal Institute of British Architects
RTHPL     Radio Times Hulton Picture Library
TBE       Trustees of the Bedford Estate
WPL       Westminster Public Library

# Index

*Bold entries indicate illustrations*